Perfect One-Dish Meals

QUARRY

Ingredients for Indian Peppered-Pork Medallions, page 116

Stilton and Sweet Onion Pie with Black Forest Ham, page 44

Shrimp and Mango Pad Thai with Cashews, page 112

Creole Shrimp and Sausage Gumbo, page 24

Smoked Chicken and Bacon Noodle Soup, page 26

Asparagus and Mascarpone Chicken Roulades, page 88

GLOUCESTER MASSACHUSETTS

QUARRY BOOKS

50 New Tastes for
Old-Fashioned Comfort Food

Perfect One-Dish Meals

Dwayne Ridgaway

First published in the United States of America by
Quarry Books, a member of
Quayside Publishing Group
33 Commercial Street
Gloucester, Massachusetts 01930-5089
Telephone: (978) 282-9590
Fax: (978) 283-2742
www.rockpub.com

Library of Congress Cataloging-in-Publication Data
Ridgaway, Dwayne.
    Perfect one-dish meals : 50 new tastes for old-fashioned comfort food /
Dwayne Ridgaway.
        p.   cm.
    Includes index.
    ISBN 1-59253-236-5 (pbk.)
    1. One-dish meals. 2. Make-ahead cookery. I. Title.
    TX840.O53R53 2006
    641.8'2—dc22   2005025543
                                                             CIP

ISBN 1-59253-236-5

10 9 8 7 6 5 4 3 2 1

Design: Wilson Harvey
Layout and Production: Q2A Solutions
Cover Image and Photography: Allan Penn Photography

Printed in Singapore

Red Curry Chicken Casserole, page 120

To culinary students everywhere who have chosen this field as their passion and dream.

I also dedicate this book to my chef instructors and professors who shared their knowledge and craft at Johnson and Wales University.

Thank you.

Contents

Salmon and Smoked Shrimp Chowder, page 28   Spring Vegetable Lasagna with Herbed Cream, page 54   Chicken and Broccoli Casserole with Biscuit Lattice, page 34

Introduction

It wasn't long ago that kitchens everywhere were alive with the activity of the day's meal preparation. It seems that those days are gone now, and today's kitchen is merely a drop point for office work, homework, and your car keys. Time has certainly changed not only what we eat, but how much we eat and when and how fast we eat it—more times than not, on the go.

I believe with every year there are more and more hours taken out of our days. Call it a government conspiracy or simply (and more logically) a hectic lifestyle that requires 80 percent more out of the day than was required years ago. With work and kids, projects and deadlines, life has become more and more hectic—and the kitchen and our stomachs suffer.

We have been thrust so far into a hectic, on-the-go lifestyle that we forget to make time for eating well, not to mention actually taking the time to prepare a good, home-cooked meal. I can certainly appreciate a hectic lifestyle and know that sometimes (if not most of the time) the last thing you want to do after a terribly long and grueling day at work is cook a five-course meal for the family, friends, or even yourself. So, I have worked diligently to develop these dishes, combining great ingredients into beautiful and delicious make-ahead one-dish meals.

Don't close the book yet. I know that one-dish meals can rustle up sour memories of time-honored dishes like Grandma's tuna casserole, but in today's kitchens, one-dish meals can be healthy, colorful, tasty, and easy to prepare. We are going to think outside of the box (or the dish) and explore some interesting combinations of flavors and textures while encouraging good, healthy eating and maintaining ease of preparation. The idea is that even with our insane lifestyles, we can still manage to make the most out of a meal. Maybe not seven days a week, but certainly more than we currently do.

The microwave has taken center stage in modern kitchens, limiting us to boxed, prepared foods that provide hardly any nutritional substance with hardly any "real" flavor. The freezer aisle grows larger every year, packed with every choice you can think of, leaving little to the culinary imagination anymore. The kitchen deserves a comeback, a revitalization of good, home-cooked meals. Success will be measured in beforehand preparation and the make-ahead-ability of the dishes. Most of my dishes here will be prepared in advance and baked later and will serve many, either for one meal or as leftovers. From soups and stews to crusty pies and casseroles, there are endless ways to take your favorite ingredients and make them into a make-ahead entrée for the family. Cooking a good, hearty, and healthy meal does not have to consume a weekend or hours in a day. Making one-dish meals utilizes your time when you have it, saving time later when you need.

Spring Greens with Ham and Gruyère Quiche, page 38

Ingredients

A one-dish meal's main purpose is to save time, effort, and pots and pans during the cooking process. Life is a busy proposition with a tremendous amount expected out of every day. Saving time in the kitchen is a healthy approach to eliminating stress. The ingredients in one-dish meals are just as important as the time saved. The approach to ingredients must still focus on freshness and good-quality items, but whenever a prepared item or frozen or canned convenience ingredient can be used, I recommend that you do so. I will admit that I rarely use canned, prepared food items, because I tend to enjoy making sauces and stocks myself; however, this is a time-consuming effort that not

everyone can afford. So, throughout these pages, my recipes include prepared stocks and broths for sauces, as well as convenience items such as canned soups and sauces. What I have discovered is shelves full of prepared items that make cooking that much easier and that much closer to a finished meal. Now, don't think this gets you off the hook and eliminates fresh vegetables and meats. These items are important for overall flavor and healthiness of the dishes. The bottom line is, when you can save time in the kitchen, do it; buy pre-chopped vegetables if you can, and use good-quality packaged stocks and sauces if you must. But remember, these convenience items come with a cost. Purchasing previously chopped

vegetables and shredded carrots and such can be much more costly than preparing them yourself, but what I have found is that the freshness is the same, unless of course you are lucky enough to have farmers' markets or stands nearby. Now, a brief note on ingredients by type:

[Meat]
For any one-dish meal, the sky is really the limit. Beef, lamb, poultry, and pork are, of course, all allowed and in many variations. One-dish meals accommodate anything—cubed, ground, chopped, steaks, or medallions. In today's markets, look for buffalo, venison, and ostrich as alternatives to beef and lamb. As I note in all of my books, my recipes are a springboard for your creativity— if you wish to substitute buffalo for the ground beef in a shepherd's pie, I encourage the change.

The important factor for meat and poultry in your meals is freshness. Using very fresh, butcher-quality meat allows you to prepare a dish ahead of time, refrigerate it for a day or two or freeze it, and bake it later. The fresher the meat, the longer the time you have to keep it before serving it.

Cuts of meat affect your meal in the amount of cooking time required. Beef especially is available in an overwhelming

variety of cuts that can sometimes be confusing. Rely on your butcher or supermarket meat counter to steer you in the right direction. Many times, the meat package will include a label indicating the best cooking method for the particular cut. For example, tenderloin and loin steaks are perfect for the grill and pan searing. Roasts and shoulder-cut meats are generally better for roasting and braising, where a longer cooking time is required. All of the recipes here give specific instruction as to what cut of meat to use, but whenever in doubt, ask the butcher.

[Vegetables]
I am lucky enough to have many farmers' markets and roadside produce stands in my area as well as the yard space to plant my own garden, so fresh vegetables are a staple in my kitchen. If this is your scenario as well, I encourage you to use excellent-quality, farm-fresh vegetables whenever you can. I find, too, that so many supermarkets and specialty gourmet stores today abound with fresh and organic produce, much of which comes from local growers in your region. As I mentioned before, whenever you can use convenience items that save you time, do so, but

try not to sacrifice quality. In most supermarkets, the selection of "prepared" or "convenience" items in the produce section is always expanding, with cut onions, pepper, celery, and carrots; shredded carrots and cabbage; prepared stir-fry blends; and salad greens. The choices are becoming increasingly more pleasing. Take advantage of these items when they look their freshest to save you valuable time in the kitchen. Many times in recipes, I will use frozen items when I know that they are adequate for a dish. For example, in baked savory pies like pot pies and shepherd's pie, I will use canned or frozen vegetables because the cooking time is long, so the vegetables are going to be cooked down

significantly. If these items are easier for you and more readily available, then use them when necessary.

[Cheese]

When thinking of one-dish meals, one's mind goes toward casseroles and savory pies, so I have developed many recipes that explore these dishes, several of which incorporate cheese as an ingredient. The key to cheese for one-dish baking is good melting ability. Cheddar, provolone, American, Gruyère, mozzarella, and Monterey Jack all have good meltability (new word for you). This means these all melt well in the dish, creating almost a sauce with the juices of the other ingredients. Feta cheese, goat cheese, and Swiss cheese tend to keep their shape when melting and don't spread

out as much as the others already listed. This is okay when it is necessary, but when looking for a smooth, creamy consistency from your cheese, the melting ones are recommended. Another important factor to consider when choosing a cheese is flavor. When looking for the cheese to impart a robust, hearty flavor to a dish, you will want to use a well-aged, sharper cheese like Parmigiano-Reggiano or sharp Cheddar.

[Bread Crumbs]

Many casserole and savory pie recipes include bread crumbs as a topping or binder in the ingredients. Whenever possible, I like to make my own fresh bread crumbs, but the reality of this is that it is time consuming. So, again, use good-quality packaged items when available. Bread crumbs are found in many varieties, whether plain or seasoned, and from many manufacturers. Find one you trust and like and stick with it. I have found that the 4C and Progresso brands offer a good, consistent product. It goes without saying, however, that making them fresh is better. When you have that day-old baguette from dinner the night before, just allow it to get hard and crunchy, break it up into the bowl of a food processor fitted with the blade attachment, and

pulse into fine crumbs. Store your homemade bread crumbs in an airtight container for weeks, using as you need them.

[Crust and Toppings]

In the Tarts, Pies, and Crusty Dishes chapter of this book, you will find several recipes for crusts and toppings, whether mashed potatoes, bread crumbs, or pie crusts. All of them are simple and provide great flavor and texture to a savory dish. Making crust for a dish is a simple procedure that not only serves a purpose but also gives a beautiful, decorative element to your savory pie or tart. If you break down the use of crust scientifically, you will see that whether a bottom crust only is used or a bottom and top crust are paired, the crust actually serves a practical purpose. Let's first discuss the double crust, or the use of a top and bottom crust. The bottom crust is there to not only add another layer of flavor and texture, but to encase the pie or tart, making it easier to serve. Without it, you have a spoon dish that is simply a casserole, not so much a quiche, tart, or savory pie. While the bottom crust is providing an element of stability to the dish, it is also absorbing a bit of the liquid from the ingredients' juices, thickening the dish during baking. The top or upper crust is again not only a flavorful

and decorative element, but it also behaves a bit like a lid or cover to the pie, keeping in the heat. The same is true for other breading or topping such as mashed potatoes or bread crumbs—a simple, effective way to keep in the heat, absorb a bit of moisture, and add a decorative element to your pie.

[Smoked Meats and Seafood]

There are a few recipes in which I use smoked meat and seafood as ingredients. Smoking foods is a tremendous way to add layers of flavor to a dish. I fell in love with the indoor technique of smoking when writing my book *Indoor Grilling*. The method is quite simple and really doesn't require any elaborate, sophisticated equipment. I use an indoor smoker by Cameron that is designed for ease of use and cleanup. You simply place specially produced wood chips in the bottom and the food item on the food rack, then slide the lid on and place on your stovetop on medium heat. Smoking times vary by ingredient type, but generally 30 minutes gets the job done. If you don't have an indoor smoker, the same effect can be achieved with a deep-sided roasting pan or a wok, a food cooling rack, and aluminum foil. For the wood chips, you must find and buy wood chips that are ground small for indoor

smoking—using regular wood chips for outdoor smoking will not work for this method. Place a large roasting pan, one large enough to accommodate your food cooling rack, over medium heat. Place about 1 or 2 tablespoons (14–28 g) of wood chips in the bottom of the pan. Using a sheet of heavy-duty aluminum foil, fold in the sides to create a drip pan with sides. Place this on your food rack; then place the food item to be smoked on the foil. Using more heavy-duty aluminum foil, cover the pan, crimping the foil tightly around the edges.

[Prepared Items]

Prepared items are essential to saving time in the kitchen, but they come at a cost. I encourage using prepared and packaged items when a recipe allows for it, keeping quality in mind. Find time-saving items that you trust and can rely on. A few items that I recommend are listed below.

Beef, chicken, or vegetable stock Ones made fresh and packaged fresh with no preservatives added to them are best.

Condensed soups Campbell's is the most recognized brand, but there may local or organic products that you prefer.

Sauces and marinades I am addicted to packaged sauces, marinades, and dressings. They are the easiest way to make a delicious, time-saving impact on a meal, as either a marinade, a sauce, or glaze.

Canned and frozen vegetables I use canned and frozen vegetable in a few recipes. I trust and enjoy frozen vegetables over canned because they are packed alone, without any liquids or sauces. However, there are recognized, trusted labels of canned vegetables that are just as good as frozen. Basically, use what you are most comfortable with if the recipe allows for it.

Exploration in Cooking Vessels: Choosing the Right Dish for One-Dish Cooking

The objective of one-dish meals is to prepare and serve the meal in one solitary dish. Now I will be the first to tell you that this is not always as easy as it sounds. But, for the most part, all the dishes in this book are capable of meeting that standard, with the exception of a few dishes that require additional cooking, sautéing, warming, or mixing in another dish, pot, or bowl. The concept overall is that you can prepare something with minimal effort and cleanup that can be served in one dish, either at the time of preparation, or later, if made ahead and stored. Concerning casseroles and savory pies and tarts, they are most often able to be fully made and refrigerated or frozen for later service. This makes it attractive to prepare meals on the weekend, when time seems to be a bit more readily available, and pull them out to serve during the week. The same goes for soups—the recipes here are intended to yield enough for leftovers during the busy days of the week. So, with that said, I list here a selection of pots and pans that serve quite well for one-dish cooking. Whether a skillet, casserole, baking dish, or wok, there is something in these pages that should appeal to everyone, also giving a bit of creative license to presentation of dishes.

[Cast Iron]

Cast iron is the grandmother of cooking vessels. Inherently nonstick due to the natural "seasoning" of the pans while cooking, and champions of heat transference, cast-iron pots and pans are readily available in a multitude of shapes, sizes, and styles. Lodge Manufacturing and Le Creuset are two widely known makers with very different approaches. Lodge offers a hardened old-world cast iron product that is black and tremendously sturdy. Considered "heirloom" quality, the Lodge cast iron pan will outlast any other product with the proper care and handling. Refer to www.lodgemfg.com for a listing of the numerous varieties of products and for instructions regarding care and keeping. Le Creuset, too, is known the world over by the finest chefs and kitchens as a leader in cast-iron cookware, but with a different niche. Le Creuset products are enamel-coated cast iron, available in a tremendous selection of sizes, shapes, and colors. The colors, I believe, are what sets Le Creuset products apart and makes them recognizable to most. Colors such as Flame, Granite, Ruby, Jade, Dune, Citrus, and Kiwi evoke feelings of European kitchens alive with activity. In addition to their cast-iron offerings, Le Creuset develops a line of enamel-coated steel stockpots and bakeware that are equally reliable and useful in the kitchen. It is important to note that when preparing a dish that will be baked or served at a later date, you should not use raw cast iron, such as the Lodge products, because of the potential for rusting. The enamel-coated products are best for this use.

[Earthenware]

Earthenware is clay bakeware that is fired at a high temperature, fusing glass particles to it, creating a sturdy, nonporous piece. Inherently, earthenware defuses heat slowly, so it is best used for dishes like soups and roasts that require a long cooking time. In addition to being practical when used in the right application, earthenware is generally decorative enough for serving in.

[Ceramic and Glass]

Ceramic and glass baking dishes are readily available and easy to use. Lasagnas, casseroles, quiches, and pies all can be baked in glass or ceramic dishes. One thing to remember: you must coat the dish with nonstick cooking spray or oil before filling to prevent sticking. Without oiling, the cleanup of a glass or ceramic dish tends to be very tedious.

[Teflon-Coated Bakeware]

Coated bakeware and cookware are always easy to clean but don't always provide the heat and even cooking I need in recipes. Years ago, I used Teflon-coated skillets and bakeware regularly, but I moved away from it in more recent years as I just miss the good browning and searing that a quality noncoated pan gives me. Also, a Teflon-coated pan prevents you from using a knife to cut and serve, an obvious drawback if you're preparing a casserole or savory pie or quiche.

[Wok]

A good wok is a necessity in every kitchen as far as I'm concerned. And most recent to the market are cast-iron woks, which I can't praise enough. The wok is probably the original one-dish cooking vessel because your entire meal is made right in this one beautiful pan. Aluminum woks are available in most housewares and kitchen stores for very reasonable prices. There is really no trick to them other than using really high heat. Gas stovetops are the best heat for this cooking application, but if you have a flat-top stove, just be sure to

buy a wok with a flat bottom so you get the best contact with the heat.

[Skillet]

A good-quality, large, ovenproof aluminum skillet is a must for good cooking. The bigger the skillet, the more you get in it. I have skillets from 5 inches (13 cm) in diameter to 17 inches (42.5 cm), and I love them all. Searing meats, then creating a sauce, and then finishing off in the oven is so easy in the right skillet. Much like a wok in that the entire meal can easily be made in them, skillets are a necessity for high-heat contact with the food.

[Baking Dish/Casserole]

Baking dishes and casseroles are designed for baking to feed a crowd or to provide intentional leftovers. Also, preparing a dish ahead of time to bake later is best achieved in baking dishes and casseroles. Many recipes in these pages are prepared and served in a baking dish, making them perfect for potluck or bake-later meals. It is important to think about the size of the vessel when cooking. I will direct you, in each recipe, to the right size dish; just be sure to stick with the size because otherwise, you will be left with either too much or too little food for your pan.

[Roasting Pan]

A roasting pan, like a good skillet, is essential in the kitchen. For the application of one-dish meals, you can prepare and bake an entire meal in one roasting pan with very little effort. A good-quality, heavy-duty pan is important because it will stand the test of time. A high-quality roasting pan is expensive but worth the investment—buy only well-recognized brands. A respected brand will stand behind the product, ensuring you get the best quality.

[Pie Dish/Tart Pan]

Integral to quiche and savory pie making are tart pans and pie plates. Coming in many shapes and sizes, tart pans are usually aluminum in construction and may or may not be Teflon coated. As previously discussed in the section on Teflon on page 13, I don't necessarily recommend Teflon in this application unless you are planning on removing the pie, tart, or quiche from the pan before cutting, because a knife will damage the Teflon. A tart is usually thin and sturdy enough to handle being removed from the pan, thus the removable bottom of tart pans. In this case, the Teflon coating comes in handy. It is recommended more for a quiche that I would use a regular glass pie plate or aluminum tart pan. Pie plates and pie dishes, too, come in varying sizes and shapes, whether deep-dish or standard. For a good, hearty quiche, I do like baking in a deep-dish pie plate—just allow for extra when making the crust.

[Stockpot/Dutch Oven]

Soups, stews, and stocks are standard one-dish meals that are great for weeklong enjoyment. Stockpots and cast-iron Dutch ovens are imperative to this cooking application. If I had to list the staples for a well-equipped kitchen, the stockpot and Dutch oven would rank right there at the top. Size is what matters when cooking in a stockpot; it is probably a good idea to have a couple of different sizes to accommodate different meals. If making a New England clam boil, bigger is better, but if making soup for four, a smaller pot will do. A solid, tight-fitting lid for locking in moisture is also important when buying a stockpot or Dutch oven.

Glossary of Terms

[Ancho Chile]
[AHN-choh] This stocky, dried chile ranges in size from 3 to 4 inches (7.5 to 10 cm) long, and has a chocolate-reddish color and a flavor from mild to pungent. The sweetest of the dried chiles, anchos have a rich, slightly fruity essence. In its fresh, green form, the ancho is referred to as a *poblano* chile.

[Andouille Sausage]
[an-DOO-ee; ahn-DWEE] A spicy, smoked sausage made from a medley of pork parts, such as chitterlings and tripe, andouille is a staple of Cajun cooking. Traditionally used in Cajun favorites such as jambalaya and gumbo, andouille makes a tasty, spicy addition to any dish calling for smoked sausage.

[Blanch]
Blanching is a technique of quickly cooking fruits and vegetables in boiling water and then "shocking" them in cold water. Blanching has many uses, some of which include loosening the skin of a fruit or vegetable for easy removal, as with peaches or tomatoes; partially cooking vegetables so they are tender, as in a vegetable crudite; and intensifying the color of a fruit or a vegetable for presentation.

[Blood Orange]
Blood oranges are distinguished by their bright red flesh and equally bright red juice, akin to a beet. Blood oranges, with a sweet-tart bite, are great eaten fresh in salads; the more acidic varieties, such as Maltese, are good in a sauce or a stir-fry. Blood oranges are the classic ingredient in the hollandaise-based sauce Maltaise.

[Braise]
[BRAYZ] A cooking method by which meats and vegetables are first browned (or seared) in butter or oil, then covered and cooked in a minimal amount of liquid (usually stock, water or wine, or a combination) over low heat for a long period of time. The long, slow cooking allows the food to tenderize while developing concentrated, intense flavor. Use a cooking vessel with a tight-fitting lid to prevent the liquid from evaporating. Braising is most commonly accomplished by first browning the food on the stove top, then moving it to the oven.

[Chipotle Chile]

[chih-POHT-lay] This hot, dried, and smoked chile begins, in its fresh state, as a jalapeño. With a characteristically wrinkled, dark-brown skin, chipotles provide a smoky, sweet, almost chocolate-like flavor to dishes. Found dried, pickled, or canned in adobo sauce, chipotles can be added to stews and sauces for intense flavor.

[Earthenware]

A favorite choice for slow-cooked dishes, earthenware is clay bakeware that is glazed with a hard, nonporous coating. Earthenware releases heat slowly, and thus is favored for dishes such as stews, roasts, roasted chicken, and roasted garlic. Earthenware is more fragile than most kitchen pots and pans, so care must be given when cooling the vessels down and when washing and storing.

[Gumbo]

[GUHM-boh] A mainstay of New Orleans cooking, gumbo is a Creole specialty with a thick, stewlike consistency that can include a tasty combination of many ingredients, such as okra, tomatoes, and onions, and one or several meats or shellfish such as chicken, sausage (the varieties of which are endless), ham, shrimp, crab, and/or oysters. The one must-have

Braised Tropical Chicken with Pineapple, Mango, and Cloves, page 104

Shrimp and Mango Pad Thai with Cashews, page 112

ingredient in all good gumbos is dark roux, which adds an unmistakable, nutty flavor. The name *gumbo* derives from the African word for "okra," which, by the way, serves to thicken the mixture during cooking.

[Jerked (Jamaican Jerk Seasoning)]

A dry seasoning blend that originated in Jamaica, jerk is used primarily in the preparation of grilled meat. The ingredients can vary, depending on the cook, but Jamaican jerk blend is generally a combination of chiles, thyme, spices (such as cinnamon, ginger, allspice, and cloves), garlic, and onions. Jerk seasoning can be either rubbed directly onto meat or blended with a liquid to create a marinade. In the Caribbean, the most common meats seasoned in this fashion are pork and chicken. Such preparations are referred to as "jerk pork" and "jerk chicken."

[Pad Thai]

The most recognized dish from Thailand, Pad Thai, in its most classic preparation, is the combination of cooked rice noodles with tofu, crushed peanuts, nam pla, bean sprouts, garlic, chiles, eggs, and shrimp, all of which are stir-fried together over high heat.

[Ponzu Sauce]

[PON-zoo] This prepared and bottled Japanese sauce is made with lemon juice or rice vinegar with soy sauce, mirin and/or sake, and kombu (seaweed), and has a classic citrus flavor. Ponzu is typically used as a condiment or dipping sauce with sushi and sashimi.

[Ragout]

[ra-GOO] A ragout is a thick, rich stew prepared with any combination of meat, poultry, or fish, with or without vegetables. Ragout finds it roots in the French verb *ragoûter*, meaning "to stimulate the appetite."

[Red Stripe Beer]

A lager beer from Jamaica found in liquor and package stores.

[Roux]

A classic thickener for sauces, soups, and stews, roux is the combination of flour and fat cooked slowly over low heat, browning the flour particles with the fat to develop a thick, paste-like consistency. Roux is defined by three classic types or colors: white, blond, and brown. The color and subsequent flavor are dependent on the length of time the roux is cooked. Both white and blond roux are used to thicken cream and white sauces; the white roux cooks just until it turns beige, and the blond, until pale golden in color. Brown roux is cooked to a deep, nutty brown, adding an intense, nutty flavor to soups, sauces, and stews. Typical in Cajun and Creole cooking, roux is a vital component for adding depth, flavor, and color to dishes such as gumbo and jambalaya.

chapter 1

Soups and Stews

[serves 6]

Red Stripe Chicken Chili

In Texas, there are literally competitions for the best chili in the state. City and state fairs are created around hundreds of pots of bubbling chili. I don't know if this is a blue ribbon–winning recipe or not, but I sure do like it. Making this one ahead of time allows the flavors to deepen.

2 tablespoons (28 ml) olive oil

1 pound (455 g) cooked chicken breast, cubed

1/2 pound (225 g) ground chorizo or diced sausage

1 medium red onion, chopped

1 small red bell pepper, chopped

1 can (4 ounces [115 g]) green chiles

1 can (15 ounces [420 g]) corn kernels, drained

1 can (15 ounces [420 g]) pink or white beans, drained and rinsed

1 bottle (12 ounces [355 ml]) Red Stripe beer

1 1/2 teaspoons (3.5 g) ground cumin

1 teaspoon (1.5 g) dried oregano

4 cups (950 ml) chicken stock

Salt and freshly cracked black pepper

2 tablespoons (8 g) chopped fresh flat-leaf parsley

1/4 cup (65 g) prepared basil pesto, for garnish

1/2 cup (55 g) shredded Gruyère cheese, for garnish

Heat olive oil in a large stockpot or cast-iron Dutch oven over medium-high heat. Add the chicken and cook until browned on all sides, about 7 minutes. Add the chorizo and cook for 3 minutes, stirring constantly. Add the onion and red pepper, cook for 4 minutes until just tender. Add the green chiles, corn kernels, and beans, cook for 3 minutes, stirring. Add beer and cook down until the foam subsides; add the cumin, oregano, and chicken stock. Bring soup to a boil, then reduce heat to low and simmer uncovered for 20 minutes. Season with salt and black pepper; add parsley, and serve, topping with a spoonful of pesto and shredded Gruyère cheese.

Beef Stew with
Potato-Chive Pancakes

A cold fall or winter day is made just right with a big bowl of piping-hot beef stew. There isn't always enough time during the week to satisfy that taste, so make this on the weekends and serve it up all week long. Wait and make the Potato-Chive Pancakes just before serving the stew for best results.

3 tablespoons (45 ml) canola or vegetable oil

2 pounds (905 g) beef sirloin, cut into 1" (2.5-cm) cubes

1 red onion, chopped

4 carrots, peeled and sliced

2 leeks, sliced thin (white parts only)

2 tablespoons (20 g) chopped fresh garlic

10 ounces (280 g) baby bella mushrooms, quartered

2 tablespoons (16 g) all-purpose flour

1 bottle (12 ounces [355 ml]) light beer

2 cups (475 ml) good-quality beef stock

1 tablespoon (15 ml) Worcestershire sauce

1 tablespoon (15 ml) steak sauce

1 teaspoon (5 ml) hot sauce

1 can (14.5 ounces [411 g]) diced tomatoes

1 tablespoon (15 ml) soy sauce

1 1/2 teaspoons (1.5 g) dried thyme

1 tablespoon (15 g) packed brown sugar

1 can (14.5 ounces [411 g]) red kidney beans, drained

1 teaspoon (6 g) salt

2 teaspoons (4 g) black pepper

1 tablespoon (8 g) cornstarch, dissolved in 1 tablespoon (15 ml) cold water

8 Potato-Chive Pancakes (recipe follows)

Heat oil in a 4-quart (3.8 L) cast-iron Dutch oven over medium-high heat. Add cubed meat and brown for 5 minutes. Using a slotted spoon, remove the meat and set aside, keeping drippings in pot. Add onion, carrots, leeks, garlic, and mushrooms; sauté until tender, about 7 minutes. Sprinkle flour over vegetables, stir to combine, cook for 3 minutes, browning the flour. Add beer and beef stock, gradually, stirring to prevent lumps. Cook until thickened. Add Worcestershire sauce, steak sauce, hot sauce, diced tomato, soy sauce, thyme, brown sugar, and beans; stir, season with salt and pepper, reduce the heat, and simmer for 20 minutes. Increase the heat, bringing the stew to a boil; add the cornstarch mixture to boiling stew, stir until thick. Cook for an additional 5 minutes; serve hot with Potato-Chive Pancakes.

POTATO-CHIVE PANCAKES

1 sweet potato, peeled

1 russet (baking) potato, peeled

1 cup (100 g) butternut squash, shredded

1 small red onion, peeled

1 egg

$^1/_4$ cup (29 g) bread crumbs

2 tablespoons (16 g) all-purpose flour

2 tablespoons (6 g) chopped fresh chives

1 tablespoon (4 g) chopped fresh flat-leaf parsley

$^1/_2$ teaspoon (3 g) salt

$^1/_2$ teaspoon (1 g) freshly ground black pepper

Vegetable oil for frying

In a food processor fitted with the shredder attachment or on the large grate of a box grater, grate the potatoes, squash, and onion into a large mixing bowl. Add the egg, bread crumbs, flour, chives, and parsley. Using your hands or a fork, combine the ingredients well to form a thick batter; season with salt and black pepper. Pour vegetable oil in skillet to a $^1/_4$" (6.25 mm) depth. Heat oil in a flat cast-iron griddle or skillet over medium-high heat; spoon potato pancake batter onto hot pan, flattening into cakes about $^1/_4$" (6.25 mm) thick; cook on both sides until browned and cooked through, about 3 to 4 minutes per side. If the cakes are cooking too fast, reduce the heat to medium. Cook in batches, keeping the cooked cakes warm.

Creole Shrimp and Sausage Gumbo

My grandmother, mother, and sister would stand in the kitchen and argue for hours over who knew the best techniques for making good gumbo. I stood by quietly, taking it all in, and little did they know that I had all the answers. The right roux leads to the best-tasting gumbo. Look to the Cook's Note for roux-making techniques.

1 cup (225 g) butter

1 cup (125 g) all-purpose flour

1/4 cup (60 ml) vegetable oil

2 cups (320 g) chopped yellow onion

1 cup (150 g) chopped green bell pepper

1/2 cup (50 g) chopped celery

4 cloves garlic, minced

1 cup (100 g) sliced fresh or frozen okra

1 can (14.5 ounces [411 g]) diced tomatoes

1 1/2 cups (355 ml) water

1 tablespoon (18 g) kosher salt

3/4 teaspoon (1.5 g) cayenne pepper

1/2 teaspoon (1.5 g) garlic powder

1/2 teaspoon (1.5 g) onion powder

1/2 teaspoon (1 g) black pepper

1/4 teaspoon (2 mg) sage, rubbed

2 cups (475 ml) vegetable or chicken stock

2 bottles (8 ounces [235 ml] each) clam juice

2 dried bay leaves

1 pound (455 g) andouille sausage, diced

1/4 cup (25 g) thinly sliced green onions

1 pound (455 g) medium shrimp, peeled and deveined

1/2 teaspoon (2.5 ml) hot sauce

4 1/2 cups (720 g) hot cooked long-grain rice

Melt the butter in a large cast-iron Dutch oven over medium-high heat. Add the flour, stirring constantly with a whisk, cooking until it is a deep, rich brown color with a nutty fragrance. Reduce the heat to medium if the flour is getting browned too fast. Remove from heat, transfer to a bowl, and set aside. To the Dutch oven add ¼ cup (60 ml) vegetable oil. Once hot, add the onion, pepper, and celery, cooking until tender, about 7 minutes. Add the garlic and cook 2 minutes; add the okra and tomatoes, cover, and cook for 5 minutes. Uncover and add the water, salt, cayenne pepper, garlic and onion powders, black pepper, sage, vegetable stock, clam juice, and bay leaves; bring to a boil. Gradually add the flour mixture (roux) in a steady stream, stirring with a whisk. Reduce the heat to a simmer and cook, uncovered, for 35 minutes, stirring occasionally. Add the sausage and cook for 10 minutes. Add the green onions and shrimp and cook for 8 minutes, until shrimp is pink and cooked through. Add the hot sauce, stirring to combine. Remove the bay leaves. Serve hot over cooked rice.

[Cook's Note]
Making Perfect Roux

Roux is simply a combination of flour and fat (butter or oil) cooked into a paste, which becomes a flavor-enhancing thickening agent. Heating the combination cooks the flour, browning it into various stages. There are three distinct roux types: white, blond, and brown. White requires the shortest cooking time and brown takes longer to cook, developing the deep brown color and nutty aroma. Roux is the main building block of a good gumbo. Typically, a brown roux is best, but there are applications that call for a milder, lighter roux. Achieving the best roux requires a cast-iron skillet and equal amounts of good-quality butter or oil and flour. For example, 1 cup (125 g) flour to 1 cup (225 g) butter or oil will produce a rich, creamy roux with thickening power. Always use a whisk to combine the two, as a spoon will not aerate the combination enough, causing lumps and burning. The longer you cook your roux, the darker and more aromatic it will become, adding depths of flavor, color, and thickness to your soup, sauce, or gravy.

Smoked Chicken and Bacon Noodle Soup

When I think of one-dish meals, I instantly think of soups and stews. Making this soup ahead of time, refrigerating, and reheating it, will intensify the flavors, resulting in a great potluck meal or an excellent dish to last multiple nights. Make a double batch and feed the family and friends for a week.

4 thick slices good-quality smoked bacon, chopped

1 tablespoon (15 ml) olive oil

1 cup (160 g) chopped sweet onion (preferably Vidalia)

1 cup (130 g) diced carrot

1 cup (100 g) sliced celery

2 cloves fresh garlic, minced

1/4 cup (30 g) all-purpose flour

1/2 teaspoon (75 mg) dried oregano

1/4 teaspoon (25 mg) dried thyme

1/4 teaspoon (2 mg) Dalmatian sage, rubbed

6 cups (1.4 L) chicken stock

4 cups (600 g) peeled and diced Yukon Gold potatoes

1 teaspoon (6 g) salt

2 cups (about 12 ounces [340 g]) shredded smoked chicken breast

1 cup (235 ml) light cream

2 cups (4 ounces [115 g]) uncooked wide egg noodles

In a large stockpot over medium-high heat, cook the bacon until browned and just crisp, about 5 minutes. Add 1 tablespoon (15 ml) olive oil, heat; add onion, carrot, celery, and garlic, sauté until just tender, 4 minutes. Sprinkle flour, dried oregano, thyme, and sage over vegetables, cooking and stirring for 3 minutes. Add chicken stock, stirring to prevent lumps. Add potatoes and salt; bring to a boil. Reduce heat to a simmer and cook for 25 minutes or until potatoes are fork tender. Add chicken, cream, and egg noodles; cook for 10 more minutes or until noodles are tender, serve.

Salmon and Smoked Shrimp Chowder

There are so many chowders that celebrate the clam. Very few pay any attention to other sea life that is well deserving of its own soup. Here, salmon and tender smoked shrimp create a glorious marriage with caramelized onions, leeks, and potatoes. Make plenty of this to serve; it is going to be well received.

5 thick slices good-quality smoked bacon, chopped

2 tablespoons (28 g) unsalted butter

1 medium onion, finely chopped

1 small fennel bulb, chopped

3 tablespoons (25 g) all-purpose flour

3 cups (710 ml) whole milk, heated

2 bottles (8 ounces [235 ml] each) clam juice

2 dried bay leaves

6-8 (about 1 pound [455 g]) boiling potatoes (small Yukon Gold), peeled and coarsely chopped

1 pound (455 g) salmon fillet, skinned, cut into large steaks

1 pound (455 g) large smoked shrimp (21/25 size)

1 cup (235 ml) light cream

1/4 cup (8 g) chopped fresh dill, loosely packed

2 teaspoons (1.2 g) dried tarragon

2 teaspoons (1.2 g) dried marjoram

Kosher salt and freshly ground black pepper

1 lime, cut into small wedges, for garnish

In a large stockpot or cast-iron Dutch oven, fry the bacon over medium-high heat, rendering the fat until the bacon is slightly crisp, 7 minutes. Add the butter to the pot and melt; add the onion and fennel and sauté until tender, 7 minutes. Sprinkle with flour, stirring to coat evenly, and cook for 2 minutes; add the warm milk and clam juice alternately, whisking after each addition. Bring to a boil; add the bay leaves and potatoes; reduce heat to low and simmer for 20 minutes, cooking the potatoes until fork tender. Add the salmon fillets and cook for 15 minutes, until the salmon is just opaque and beginning to flake. Remove salmon fillets, flake apart, and add back to the chowder. Add the shrimp, light cream, dill, tarragon, and marjoram; bring soup to boil once again; season with salt and pepper; cook for 10 minutes longer; remove bay leaves; serve hot with a lime wedge.

chapter 2

Tarts, Pies, and Crusty Dishes

[serves 6]

Buffalo Chicken Pot Pie **with** Gorgonzola-Potato Crust

Most chicken pot pie recipes seem to call for a thick crust and vegetables that lack zing. Buffalo-style chicken wings may seem overdone, but no one will ever claim they lack zip!

3 cups (710 ml) chicken stock, heated to a simmer

2 tablespoons (28 g) unsalted butter

2 medium carrots, diced

2 celery ribs, diced

1/4 cup (40 g) finely chopped shallots

2 cloves fresh garlic, minced

1/4 cup (30 g) all-purpose flour

1 dried bay leaf

1/4 teaspoon (4 mg) dried oregano

1/2 teaspoon (1.5 g) chile powder

1/4 teaspoon (6 mg) ground cumin

1/4 teaspoon (75 mg) ancho chile powder

Kosher salt and freshly ground black pepper

2 whole cooked chicken breasts, diced 3/4" (1.9 cm) thick

1 cup (210 g) thawed frozen pearl onions

1/2 cup (65 g) thawed frozen green peas

3 tablespoons (45 ml) buffalo wing sauce

POTATO CRUST

1 1/2 pounds (680 g) russet (baking) potatoes, peeled, rough chopped

3 tablespoons (45 g) butter

1/4 cup (60 g) sour cream

1/3 cup (40 g) crumbled Gorgonzola or blue cheese

2 tablespoons (28 ml) heavy cream

3 tablespoons (9 g) minced fresh chives

Salt and freshly ground black pepper to taste

10 sheets phyllo dough, thawed

Heat the stock to a simmer in a saucepan over low heat. In a large skillet, melt 2 tablespoons (28 g) butter over medium-high heat; add carrots and celery and sauté until tender, about 4 minutes. Add shallots and garlic and cook for an additional 2 minutes. Sprinkle with flour and cook for 2 minutes, until flour begins to turn golden and develop a nutty aroma. Add 1 cup (235 ml) stock, stirring vigorously to combine and prevent lumps, being cautious of the steam that rises when adding the stock. Add stock 1 cup (235 ml) at a time, stirring after each addition. Add bay leaf, oregano, chile powder, cumin, and ancho chile powder; season with salt and pepper. Add chicken, pearl onions, peas, and buffalo sauce, stirring to combine. Cook for 10 minutes, remove from heat, and set aside.

Place potatoes in a large saucepan, adding water to reach about 1" to 2" (2.5 to 5 cm) above them. Place over high heat and bring to a boil, cooking until potatoes are fork tender, about 12 minutes. Remove from heat and drain, leaving in the pot; mash potatoes with butter, sour cream, Gorgonzola, and cream. Once creamy, add chives and season with salt and black pepper. Preheat oven to 400°F (200°C, or gas mark 6); place the chicken mixture in a greased 9" x 13" (22.5 x 32.5 cm) baking casserole. Remove bay leaf. Using a piping bag or a large resealable plastic bag fitted with a large tip, pipe potato mixture in random mounds on top of the chicken mixture, covering completely.

Working with one sheet of phyllo at a time, brush thoroughly and evenly with melted butter. Crumple phyllo sheets like tissue paper on top of the potato layer. Repeat with additional sheets until top is covered.

Place on middle rack of oven, uncovered, and bake for 30 minutes, until phyllo is browned. If phyllo is browning too fast, cover loosely with aluminum foil. Serve hot.

[serves 6]

Chicken-Sausage Pies with Apple and Leeks

Chicken pot pie is traditionally baked in a large casserole dish packed with hearty, fresh ingredients and topped with a flaky pastry crust. I have kept all of the classic flavors while throwing in a twist of my own with sausage, apple, and leeks. If you don't have individual casserole dishes, one large, deep dish can also be used.

1 cup (110 g) chopped chorizo (hot or mild)

8 tablespoons (1 stick [112 g]) unsalted butter, cut into $1/2$" (1.25-cm) cubes

$1/2$ cup (80 g) chopped onion

$1/2$ cup (60 g) chopped leeks, white parts only

1 cup (150 g) peeled and chopped green apple

$1/2$ cup (75 g) chopped red-skinned potatoes

$1/2$ teaspoon (1 g) fennel seeds

$1/2$ cup (60 g) all-purpose flour

4 cups (9464 ml) chicken stock, heated over low heat

$1/2$ teaspoon (4 mg) chopped fresh thyme

1 teaspoon (1.3 g) chopped fresh tarragon

1 bay leaf

1 cup (140 g) chopped cooked chicken meat

Salt and freshly ground pepper, to taste

6 rectangles (5" x 8" [13 x 20 cm]) or discs (8" [20 cm]) frozen puff pastry

1 egg, beaten with 1 teaspoon (5 ml) water

Place a large cast-iron or aluminum pot over medium-high heat, add the chorizo, and cook until the fat begins to render and the sausage begins to brown, 4 minutes; add butter and melt. Add the onions, leeks, apple, potatoes, and fennel seeds to the pot and sauté until tender, about 7 minutes. Sprinkle with flour and stir vigorously to combine, cooking the flour until golden, about 3 additional minutes. Gradually add in the chicken stock, being careful of the steam that will rise from the pot. Stir until thick; continue adding the chicken stock, stirring after each addition to prevent lumps from forming. Once all the stock has been added, add the thyme, tarragon, and bay leaf and cook for an additional 5 minutes. Add the chicken meat, season with salt and pepper, remove from heat, and set aside. If making to refrigerate or freeze, cool the chicken filling completely and then proceed. Working with six individual 3" x 5" (7.5 x 13-cm) ovenproof dishes or six

5" (13-cm) round ovenproof dishes, spray each with nonstick cooking spray and fill three-quarters full with chicken mixture. Brush the edges of each casserole dish with the egg wash, place one rectangle or round of puff pastry on top of each dish, pressing lightly on the edges. Cut three slits in the top of the pastry to release steam; brush with egg wash. If preparing for later use, cover each tightly with plastic wrap and refrigerate for up to 2 days. Remove from refrigerator, let come to room temperature for 20 minutes. Bake at 400°F (200°C, or gas mark 6) until the pastry is puffed and golden brown, about 30 minutes. Remove and serve hot. Alternatively, for freezing, cover each dish tightly with plastic wrap and place each individually in a gallon-size freezer bag. Store in freezer for up to one month. To bake, transfer to refrigerator and thaw for 24 hours, then follow instructions above for baking.

2 tablespoons (28 ml) olive oil

1 1/2 pounds (680 g) boneless, skinless chicken breast, cut into 1/2" (1.25-cm) chunks

Salt and pepper

2 cups (about 8 ounces [225 g]) roughly chopped cremini mushrooms, stems trimmed

6 cloves fresh garlic, minced

1 can (10.75 ounces [295 g]) condensed cream of broccoli soup

1 can (10.75 ounces [295 g]) condensed cream of chicken soup

1/2 cup (120 g) sour cream

1 cup (115 g) shredded Cheddar cheese

1 cup (110 g) shredded Gruyère cheese

2 packages (10 ounces [280 g] each) frozen chopped broccoli, thawed and well drained

1 tablespoon (1.7 g) chopped fresh rosemary

1 package (11 ounces [310 g]) bake-and-serve breadsticks or biscuits

[serves 4]

Chicken and Broccoli
Casserole **with Biscuit Lattice**

This casserole is as attractive to serve as it is good to eat. With easy make-ahead preparation, this is a quick oven-to-table meal with very little prep time involved. You can also refrigerate it a day or two before baking.

Preheat oven to 375°F (190°C, or gas mark 5). Heat olive oil in a large sauté pan over medium-high heat. Add the cubed chicken, season with salt and pepper, and sauté until browned and cooked through, about 7 minutes. Add mushrooms and garlic, continue to sauté for an additional 3 minutes or until the mushrooms begin to release moisture. Remove from heat and transfer to a large bowl; add the soups, sour cream, cheeses, broccoli, and rosemary; stir to combine. Place the chicken mixture into a 9" (22.5-cm) square casserole. Working with the breadsticks, remove individual strips and begin laying them over the top of the casserole, weaving the strips in and out of each other in a basket weave configuration. At this point, either cover the casserole tightly with plastic wrap and refrigerate until ready to bake, or place on center rack of oven and bake for 35 minutes, until the bread topping is browned and baked through. Remove and serve. If refrigerating for later use, when ready to bake, remove from refrigerator and let stand for 20 minutes; bake as above. Serve warm with white or brown rice.

All-Season Quiche—Four Recipes for Seasonal Baking

One dish, one crust, and four delicious alternatives for mouthwatering quiche. On the hot days of summer or the frozen nights of winter, there is a quiche here for you. The beauty of quiche and tarts is that they can be made ahead and served at a later time or place. Quiche are perfect for weekend preparation and weekday eating or as a traveling potluck option. Cut them into squares or slices, pack them individually, and you have a perfect on-the-go meal.

STANDARD PASTRY CRUST

1¹/₄ cups (150 g) all-purpose flour

¹/₂ teaspoon (3 g) salt

1 tablespoon (5 g) freshly grated Parmesan cheese

8 tablespoons (1 stick [112 g]) chilled unsalted butter, cut into 1" (2.5-cm) pieces

1 to 2 tablespoons (15–30 ml) ice water

To make the pastry, in the bowl of an electric mixer fitted with the flat beater, or in the bowl of a food processor fitted with the blade attachment, combine the flour, salt, and Parmesan cheese; beat or pulse on low speed for 15 seconds. Add the butter and continue beating or pulsing (for the processor) until the dough is the consistency of pea-sized crumbs, 30 to 45 seconds. Add the water ¹/₂ tablespoon (8 ml) at a time and continue beating or pulsing, adding more water as needed, until the dough comes together, pulling away from the sides of the bowl.

Turn the dough out onto a lightly floured surface and press together to form a 5" (13-cm) disk, being careful not to overwork the dough. Cover with plastic wrap and refrigerate for at least 1 hour, or until ready to use.

Spring Greens with Ham and Gruyère Quiche, page 38

Summer Tomato and Basil with Buffalo Mozzarella and Feta Quiche, page 39

Fall Fennel and Sausage Quiche, page 40

Winter Potato and Bacon with Leeks and Thyme Quiche, page 41

Spring Greens with Ham and Gruyère Quiche

1 recipe Standard Pastry Crust (page 36)

2 tablespoons (28 ml) extra-virgin olive oil

2 shallots, chopped

2 cloves garlic, minced

2 leeks, white parts sliced thin

1 tablespoon (15 g) sugar

1/2 pound (225 g) baby spinach, coarsely chopped

1 bunch watercress, rinsed, thoroughly drained, coarsely chopped

1 bunch fresh Italian arugula, rinsed, drained, coarsely chopped

2 eggs

1/2 cup (120 ml) milk

1/4 cup (60 ml) heavy cream

1/2 cup (120 ml) good-quality chicken stock

Salt and freshly ground black pepper

1/2 cup (about 6 ounces [170 g]) chopped thickly sliced Black Forest ham

1/4 cup (15 g) rough-chopped flat-leaf parsley

1/4 cup (10 g) rough-chopped fresh basil

2 tablespoons (6 g) chopped fresh chives

2 tablespoons (8 g) chopped fresh tarragon

1 cup (110 g) shredded Gruyère cheese

1/4 cup (30 g) shredded mozzarella cheese

Remove the pastry dough from the refrigerator. Roll it out on a lightly floured work surface to about 1/8" (3 mm) thick to conform to a 9" (22.5-cm) square tart pan. Press the dough into the bottom and up the sides of the pan; trim the dough, leaving a 1/2" (1.25-cm) overhang around the sides. Fold in the excess, pressing into the sides so they are thicker than the bottom. Cover with plastic wrap and chill for 30 minutes. Preheat the oven to 375°F (190°C, or gas mark 5). Line the dough with a sheet of aluminum foil or parchment paper and cover with pastry weights or large dried beans or raw rice. Place the dough on the center rack of the oven and bake for 20 minutes, remove the foil and weights, and bake for an additional 5 minutes, until the dough is set and golden. Remove from oven and place on a wire cooling rack to cool.

In a large skillet, heat the olive oil over medium-high heat.

Add the shallots and garlic, sauté for 2 minutes; add the leeks and cook for an additional 4 minutes, until just wilted. Sprinkle with sugar; reduce heat to low, and cook until the leeks are a rich, golden color, 8 minutes. Add spinach, watercress, and arugula, tossing to wilt, about 3 minutes. Remove from heat and set aside to cool. In a mixing bowl, whisk together the eggs, milk, and heavy cream; add the chicken stock and season with salt and black pepper. Begin assembling the quiche. Sprinkle the ham in the bottom of the crust, top with the fresh herbs, mixing them together with each addition. Add the wilted spinach and leek mixture, then the shredded cheeses, and pour the whipped egg mixture over. Place in the hot oven and bake until set and golden, about 45 minutes. Remove from the oven and let rest for 5 minutes, slice, and serve or cool completely and refrigerate for later service.

Summer Tomato and Basil with Buffalo Mozzarella and Feta Quiche

CRUST ALTERNATIVE

To the Standard Pastry Crust (page 36) add $1/2$ teaspoon (1 g) freshly ground black pepper to spice up the flavors.

1 recipe Standard Pastry Crust (page 36)

4 tablespoons (60 ml) extra-virgin olive oil, divided

2 cloves garlic, minced

8 ounces (225 g) fresh buffalo mozzarella, sliced thin

2 tablespoons (10 g) freshly grated Parmigiano-Reggiano cheese

$1/4$ cup (10 g) fresh basil, chopped

2 pounds (905 g) heirloom or vine-ripened tomatoes, sliced about $1/4$" (6.25 mm) thick

6 ounces (170 g) crumbled feta cheese

Heat 2 tablespoons (28 ml) olive oil in a small skillet over medium-high heat, add the garlic, and sauté for 2 minutes, just to remove the bitter flavor. Remove from heat and set aside. Place the buffalo mozzarella in an overlapping layer in the bottom of the tart shell, then sprinkle with garlic and Parmigiano-Reggiano cheese. Top with basil (reserving 1 tablespoon [2.5 g] for the top) and then the tomatoes in an overlapping layer. Dot the tomatoes with the crumbled feta cheese, drizzle with remaining 2 tablespoons (28 ml) olive oil, and bake for 30 minutes, until the tart is set and the tomatoes are beginning to brown on top. Remove, let rest 5 minutes, sprinkle with reserved basil, and serve.

Preheat the oven to 375°F (190°C, or gas mark 5). On a lightly floured surface, roll out the dough to $1/8$" (3-mm) thickness to fit a $13^3/4$" x $4^1/4$" (35- x 11-cm) rectangular tart pan. Press the dough into the pan; trim, leaving a $1/2$" (1.25-cm) overhang around the rim. Fold in the excess dough and press it into the sides so they are thicker than the bottom. Refrigerate for at least 10 minutes. Cover the dough with aluminum foil or parchment paper and line with pastry weights or dried beans or rice. Bake on the center rack of the oven for 20 minutes, remove foil or parchment, and bake for an additional 5 minutes, until golden; remove and let cool.

Fall Fennel and Sausage Quiche

1 recipe Standard Pastry Crust (page 36)

1 large fennel bulb

2 tablespoons (30 ml) olive oil

1/2 cup (80 g) chopped yellow onion

3 cloves garlic, minced

1/2 cup (75 g) diced smoked ham

1/2 pound (225 g) chorizo or sweet Italian sausage, sliced on the diagonal about 1/4" (6.25 mm) thick

1 teaspoon (8 mg) chopped fresh thyme

1/2 teaspoon (4 mg) chopped fresh savory

1 teaspoon (2.5 g) paprika

1 tablespoon (4 g) chopped flat-leaf parsley

Salt and freshly ground black pepper, to taste

1 egg white

2 eggs

1 cup (235 ml) milk

1/4 cup (60 ml) heavy cream

1/4 cup (30 g) shredded provolone cheese

1/4 cup (30 g) shredded Swiss cheese

1/2 teaspoon (3 g) salt

1/2 teaspoon (1 g) freshly cracked black pepper

2 tablespoons (10 g) freshly grated Parmigiano-Reggiano cheese

Remove the pastry dough from the refrigerator. Roll it out on a lightly floured work surface to about 1/8" (3 mm) thick to form an 11" (27.5-cm) circle. Press the dough into the bottom and up the sides of a 10" (25-cm) tart pan with removable bottom. Cover with plastic wrap and chill for 30 minutes. Preheat the oven to 375°F (190°C, or gas mark 5). Prick the bottom of the crust with a fork in a few places to prevent bubbling during baking. Line the dough with a sheet of aluminum foil or parchment paper and cover with pastry weights or large dried beans or raw rice. Place the dough on the center rack of the oven and bake for 20 minutes, remove the foil and weights, and bake for an additional 5 minutes until the dough is set and golden. Remove from oven and place on a wire cooling rack to cool.

Strip the outer, brown leaves from the fennel bulb and cut the bulb vertically into quarters. Cutting in a wedge, remove the tough inner core from the quarters. Slice each quarter horizontally into thin strips. Heat the olive oil in a large skillet over medium-high heat. Once hot, add the fennel and onion, sauté until tender and they begin to turn golden, 7 minutes. Add the garlic and the ham and sauté for 2 minutes; add the sausage and cook for 5 minutes, until the sausage begins to sweat and brown. Remove from the heat. While still hot, stir in the thyme, savory, paprika, and parsley; season with salt and black pepper, set aside to cool. In a large bowl, whisk together the egg white, eggs, milk, and cream; add the provolone and Swiss cheese; season with salt and pepper, stirring to combine. Scoop the fennel/sausage mixture into the bottom of the crust, spreading into an even layer. Pour the egg mixture over and even out. Sprinkle with Parmigiano Reggiano cheese and bake for 35 to 45 minutes, until puffed and golden. Remove from oven, let rest for 10 minutes, serve hot or refrigerate to reheat for later service. When reheating, cover with aluminum foil to protect the top from burning. Reheat at 350°F (180°C, or gas mark 4) for about 30 minutes.

Winter Potato and Bacon with Leeks and Thyme Quiche

1 recipe Standard Pastry Crust (page 36)

5 slices thick-cut smoked bacon, chopped

1 tablespoon (15 g) butter

1 large yellow onion, sliced

2 leeks, white parts only, cut in half lengthwise, washed, and sliced thin

1 teaspoon (8 mg) finely chopped fresh thyme, divided

Salt and freshly ground pepper

1 large (about $3/4$ pound [340 g]) russet potato, parboiled for 7–10 minutes, cooled and cut crosswise into slices $1/8$" (3 mm) thick

2 eggs, lightly beaten

$1/2$ cup (120 ml) heavy cream

1 tablespoon (15 ml) olive oil

Remove the pastry dough from the refrigerator. Roll it out on a lightly floured work surface to about $1/8$" (3 mm) thickness to fit tart pan (either $13\frac{3}{4}$" x $4\frac{1}{4}$" (35- x 11-cm) rectangular or a 9" (22.5-cm) square). Press the dough into the bottom and up the sides of the pan; trim the dough, leaving a $1/2$" (1.25-cm) overhang around the sides. Fold in the excess, pressing into the sides so they are thicker than the bottom. Cover with plastic wrap and chill for 10 minutes. Preheat the oven to 400°F (200°C, or gas mark 6). Place the oven rack in the bottom third of the oven. In a large skillet over medium-high heat, fry the bacon, rendering the fat, until just browned and crisp; transfer to a paper towel to drain, leaving the grease behind in the pan. To the skillet add the butter and melt. Add the onion and leeks, sauté until just tender, about 5 minutes. Reduce the heat to low, add $1/2$ teaspoon (.4 g) thyme, and continue to cook for 10 minutes, until the onion and leek begin to brown and become caramelized. Remove the pan from the heat, season with salt and pepper, and stir in the potatoes; let cook for 5 minutes. In a small bowl, beat the eggs with the heavy cream; add to the potato mixture, stirring to combine. Brush the pastry dough with the olive oil and pour the quiche mixture into the tart pan. Place in the oven and bake until set, 50 to 60 minutes. Remove, sprinkle with remaining $1/2$ teaspoon (.4 g) thyme, let cool on a wire rack for at least 10 minutes, slice, and serve.

A **World of** Shepherd's Pie—
Four Variations on a Classic

While researching shepherd's, cottage, and other hearty pies,
I came upon a book, *The Art of the Tart*, that was intriguing,
educational, and fun to read and look at. The author, Tamasin
Day-Lewis, a well-respected and well-regarded food writer, has
compiled a delightful combination of savory and sweet pies and
hearty dishes. I was inspired by a few of them for these
"worldly" versions of shepherd's pie, typically, to me,
a New England dish. I didn't want to shortchange my readers
with just one prejudicial pie recipe, so I compiled four that
seem to take ingredients and flair from different parts of the
globe, with a bit of English-countryside influence to them all.

Stilton and Sweet Onion Pie with Black Forest Ham, page 44

New England–Inspired Shepherd's Pie with Cheddar Mashed Potatoes, page 45

Italian Cottage Pie, page 46

Fish and Scallop Pie, page 47

Stilton and Sweet Onion Pie with Black Forest Ham

3¼ pounds (1.5 kg) russet potatoes (or other starchy potato), peeled and quartered

4 medium yellow onions

8 tablespoons (112 g) unsalted butter, divided

3 cloves garlic, minced

²/₃ cup (160 ml) milk

1 bunch Swiss chard, tough stems removed, coarsely chopped

Freshly ground black pepper

½ pound (225 g) Stilton cheese, crumbled

¾ cup (about ¼ pound, or 115 g) thickly sliced smoked ham, chopped into ¼" (6.25-mm) dice

¼ cup (25 g) freshly grated Parmesan cheese

Cook the potatoes in a large pot of boiling water until tender, about 15 minutes. Meanwhile, peel the onions and cut in half vertically, and then cut each half into 5 or 6 wedges. In an 11" or 12" (27.5- or 30-cm) cast-iron or other heavy-bottomed skillet, melt 3 tablespoons (45 g) butter over low to medium heat, add the onions, and cook, stirring occasionally, for 20 to 25 minutes until soft and caramelized. Transfer the onions to a plate. To the same skillet, add 3 tablespoons (45 g) butter and melt over medium heat. Once the butter is melted, add the garlic and cook until just tender and beginning to brown, about 5 minutes; remove from heat and set aside. In a small saucepot, bring the milk to boil; then remove from heat and set aside. Drain the potatoes and transfer to the bowl of a mixer fitted with the paddle. Mix on low, adding the milk and butter-and-garlic mixture gradually,

beating to a smooth mash. In the same skillet, melt the remaining 2 tablespoons (28 g) butter. Add the Swiss chard and cook until just wilted, about 3 minutes. Remove and set aside to cool. Preheat the oven to 400°F (200°C, or gas mark 6). Spoon half of the mashed potatoes into the same cast-iron or heavy-bottomed skillet used earlier, smoothing them out evenly; then add the Swiss chard and onions in even layers and sprinkle with black pepper. Crumble the Stilton over the onions, add the ham evenly, and add the remaining mashed potatoes over the top, smoothing lightly with the back of a spoon or rubber spatula. Dust the top with grated Parmesan cheese and bake for 25 to 30 minutes, until the top is golden and the filling is bubbling. Remove, let stand for 5 minutes, and serve.

New England–Inspired Shepherd's Pie with Cheddar Mashed Potatoes

1/4 cup (60 ml) olive oil

1 large yellow onion, chopped

1 large carrot, finely chopped

1 large parsnip, finely chopped

3 cloves garlic, chopped

1/2 cup (45 g) chopped white cabbage

1 large turnip, chopped

1 1/2 pounds (680 g) ground lamb or beef

1 tablespoon (15 g) tomato paste

1 cup (235 ml) red wine

1 cup (235 ml) beef stock

2 1/4 pounds (1 kg) russet or Idaho potatoes, peeled and chopped

3 tablespoons (45 g) butter, plus 2 tablespoons (28 g) cut into pieces

3 tablespoons (45 g) sour cream

3 tablespoons (45 ml) heavy cream

2 tablespoons (6 g) chopped fresh chives

2 tablespoons (8 g) chopped fresh parsley

Sea salt and black pepper

1 cup (115 g) shredded Cheddar cheese

2 teaspoons (10 ml) Worcestershire sauce

3 dashes Tabasco

1 can (14 ounces, or 400 g) creamed corn

1 package (10 ounces, or 280 g) frozen peas, thawed

In a large skillet, heat the olive oil over medium heat. Once hot, add the onion, carrot, parsnip, and garlic to the skillet. Sauté the vegetables in the oil until tender, about 10 minutes. Add the cabbage and turnip and cook for 5 minutes longer. Increase the heat to high and add the meat, cooking until browned all around. Add the tomato paste, red wine, and stock, cooking and stirring until the liquid is absorbed and reduced by half. Meanwhile, bring the potatoes to boil in a large pot of water; cook until tender, about 15 minutes. Remove and transfer to a large mixing bowl. Using a potato masher or ricer, mash the potatoes while still hot, with the butter, sour cream, heavy cream, chives, and parsley. Season with salt and pepper, add the Cheddar cheese, stir, and set aside. Add the Worcestershire sauce and Tabasco to the meat mixture, season with salt and black pepper. Preheat the oven to 400°F (200°C, or gas mark 6). Place the corn in the bottom of a 2-quart (1.9-L) casserole dish. Top with meat mixture, then sprinkle peas over evenly. Scoop the mashed potatoes over the top, smooth out with the back of a wooden spoon or rubber spatula, ruffle with a fork, and dot with the remaining 2 tablespoons (28 g) of butter. Cook for 10 minutes to brown the potatoes a bit, then reduce the heat to 350°F (180°C, or gas mark 4) and cook for an additional 45 minutes. If you wish the top to be more brown and toasted, turn the oven to the broiler and broil for a few minutes.

Italian Cottage Pie

2¹/₄ pounds (1 kg) russet or Idaho potatoes, peeled and chopped

3 tablespoons (45 g) butter

¹/₄ cup (60 ml) milk

3 tablespoons (15 g) grated Parmesan cheese

¹/₂ cup (2 ounces, or 60 g) grated provolone cheese

Salt and freshly ground black pepper

2 tablespoons (8 g) chopped fresh parsley

1 recipe Bolognese Meat Sauce (recipe follows)

1 can (28 ounces [785 ml]) diced tomatoes with basil

Bring the potatoes to boil in a large pot of water; cook until tender, about 15 minutes. Remove and transfer to a large mixing bowl. Using a potato masher or ricer, mash the potatoes while still hot, with the butter, milk, Parmesan cheese, and provolone cheese. Season with salt and black pepper, add parsley, stir, and set aside. Preheat oven to 400°F (200°C, or gas mark 6). Place the meat sauce in the bottom of a 2-quart (1.9-L) casserole dish, topping with the tomatoes in an even layer. Spoon the mashed potatoes on top, smoothing with the back of a spoon or rubber spatula, creating ripples as you go. Bake at 400°F (200°C, or gas mark 6) for 10 to 15 minutes, just until the potatoes are browning. Reduce the heat to 350°F (180°C, or gas mark 4) and continue to bake for 45 minutes, until the potatoes are crisp and browned. Remove and let rest for 5 minutes; serve hot.

BOLOGNESE MEAT SAUCE

Makes 4 cups (1 L)

2 tablespoons (28 ml) olive oil

2 tablespoons (14 g) butter

²/₃ cup (150 g) minced beef

²/₃ cup (150 g) minced pork

²/₃ cup (150 g) minced veal

¹/₂ cup (75 g) prosciutto, finely chopped

1 large onion, chopped

1 medium carrot, peeled and chopped

2 stalks celery, cleaned and chopped

3 garlic cloves, crushed

2 sprigs flat-leaf parsley, finely chopped

1 bay leaf, crumbled

¹/₂ teaspoon (15 mg) fresh rosemary, finely chopped

1 cup (225 ml) beef stock

1 medium ripe tomato, peeled, seeded, and chopped

2¹/₄ cups (225 g) fresh mushrooms, sliced

1 cup (235 ml) dry red wine

1 cup (235 ml) dry red wine

1 cup (235 ml) milk

¹/₄ teaspoon (2 mg) nutmeg

In a large stockpot, heat the olive oil and melt the butter. Brown the beef, pork, veal and prosciutto. Add the onion, carrot, celery, garlic, parsley, bay leaf, and rosemary, and cook on medium heat for 10 minutes. Add the beef stock and tomatoes. Cook for 5 minutes. Add the mushrooms and cook for an additional 5 minutes. Increase the heat to medium-high, add the red wine and cook for 2 minutes until the smell of wine subsides. Add milk and nutmeg, and reduce heat to a gentle simmer. Simmer uncovered for 1¹/₂ to 2 hours until thick and hearty, stirring occasionally.

[serves 6]

Fish and Scallop Pie

1 pound (455 g) Yukon Gold potatoes, peeled

1 pound (455 g) sweet potatoes, peeled

3 tablespoons (45 g) unsalted butter

3 tablespoons (45 ml) heavy cream

Salt and freshly ground black pepper

2 pounds (905 g) cod, skinned and filleted

1 1/2 cups (355 ml) milk

1/2 pound (225 g) smoked salmon

1/4 cup (55 g) unsalted butter

3 leeks, white part only, cleaned and cut into rings

2 carrots, peeled and chopped

2 shallots, minced

1/4 cup (30 g) all-purpose flour

1 cup (235 ml) dry vermouth

1 bay leaf

1/8 teaspoon (6 mg) grated nutmeg

8 large sea scallops, cleaned and cut in half horizontally

1 bunch fresh dill, chopped

Preheat the oven to 400°F (200°C, or gas mark 6). Bring the potatoes and sweet potatoes to a boil in a large pot of salted water; cook until fork tender, about 20 minutes. Drain potatoes, place back in pot, add 3 tablespoons (45 g) butter and heavy cream. Using a fork or potato masher, mash the potatoes to a creamy consistency, season with salt and black pepper, and set aside. Place the cod in a 1-quart (9,464-ml) gratin pan; pour the milk over the fish. Place the fish in the oven and bake for 20 minutes. Remove from oven (the fish may be undercooked—that is okay). Transfer fish to a plate, reserving the milk. Remove any bones and skin from the fish, and flake the fish back into the gratin dish. Flake the smoked salmon into the gratin dish. Set aside. In a separate large skillet, melt 1/4 cup (55 g) butter over medium-high heat. Add the leeks, carrots, and shallots and sauté until tender, about 8 minutes. Sprinkle with the flour and whisk until a nutty aroma permeates the air and the flour, or roux, is beginning to turn light brown, about 5 minutes. Gradually add the reserved warm milk to the roux, whisking vigorously to prevent lumps. Add the vermouth, bay leaf, and grated nutmeg; cook for 10 minutes, until cooked down by half. Season well with salt and black pepper. Reduce the oven temperature to 350°F (180°C, or gas mark 4). Add the raw scallops to the gratin pan with the fish. Remove the bay leaf from the leek mixture, stir in the dill, and then pour over the fish mixture. Cover the casserole with the mashed potatoes, using the fork to ruffle the potatoes along the top. Place dish on a sheet pan and bake for about 30 minutes, until the sauce begins to bubble through the potatoes and the potatoes begin to turn brown. Serve hot.

chapter 3

Classic Casseroles and Baked Lasagnas

Swiss Baked Chicken and Ham
Casserole **with Bread Crumbs**

Years ago, my mother made a delicious baked chicken and ham dish that would easily feed us for a couple of days. When you don't have enough time to create your own sauces and stocks from scratch, canned soups come in handy. Try mixing things up in this recipe, altering the ingredients to satisfy your own particular tastes.

1 can (10.75 ounces [295 g]) cream of chicken soup	1 cup (115 g) seasoned bread crumbs
1 can (10.75 ounces [295 g]) cream of mushroom soup	2 tablespoons (10 g) grated Parmesan cheese
1/2 cup (120 g) sour cream	6 (6-ounce [170 g]) boneless, skinless chicken breasts
1/4 cup (60 ml) chicken stock	
2 teaspoons (10 g) Dijon mustard	6 thick-cut slices (about 1/4 pound [115 g]) deli roasted ham
1 teaspoon (1.5 g) dried oregano	6 slices deli Swiss cheese
1 tablespoon (4 g) chopped fresh flat-leaf parsley	4 tablespoons (55 g) butter, softened
1/2 teaspoon (1 g) freshly ground black pepper	

Preheat oven to 375°F (190°C, or gas mark 5). Grease the bottom and sides of a 9" x 13" (22.5 x 32.5 cm) baking dish; set aside. In a large mixing bowl, combine the soups with the sour cream, chicken stock, Dijon mustard, oregano, parsley, and black pepper. In a separate, smaller bowl, combine the bread crumbs with the Parmesan cheese. Place the chicken breasts in one even layer in the bottom of the baking dish; pour the soup mixture over, spreading to coat the chicken evenly. Top each breast with a slice of ham and a slice of Swiss cheese, sprinkle entire dish evenly with bread crumb mixture, dot randomly with butter, and place on the center rack of the oven. Bake until the sauce is bubbly, cheese is melted, and the internal temperature of the chicken is 165°F (75°C), about 45 minutes. Remove and serve hot with steamed vegetables, pasta, or rice.

Roasted Asparagus Lasagna with Fontina Cheese

Fresh, oven-roasted asparagus is a favorite of mine with any dish. In this lasagna, I have combined the rich flavors of Parmigiano cream sauce and Fontina cheese with the intense flavors of roasted asparagus and onions.

2¹/2 pounds [1.15 kg] medium asparagus, ends trimmed, stalks peeled, and cut in half

1 large Vidalia or sweet onion, peeled, cut in half, and thinly sliced

3 tablespoons [41 ml] extra-virgin olive oil

2 tablespoons (28 g) unsalted butter

¹/4 cup (60 ml) fresh-squeezed lemon juice

2 teaspoons (5 g) grated lemon peel

Salt

Coarsely ground black pepper

3 fresh savory sprigs, leaves removed and chopped

2 fresh tarragon sprigs, leaves removed and chopped

PARMIGIANO SAUCE

1 cup (100 g) freshly grated Parmigiano-Reggiano cheese

2 cups (475 ml) heavy cream

Freshly grated nutmeg

3 tablespoons (7.5 g) fresh chives, finely chopped

1 pound (455 g) dry lasagna noodles

¹/2 pound (100 g) grated Fontina cheese

¹/2 pound (100 g) grated mozzarella cheese

Preheat the oven to 450°F (230°C, or gas mark 8). Place the asparagus and onions on a large baking sheet. Drizzle with the olive oil, and dot with the butter. Sprinkle the lemon juice and zest on top and season with salt and coarsely ground black pepper. Mix the vegetables well with your hands, making sure they are evenly coated with the seasonings. Bake until soft and just starting to brown, about 20 minutes.

When the vegetables are tender and aromatic, remove them from the oven and sprinkle with the savory and tarragon. Toss to combine. The heat of the vegetables will wilt and concentrate the flavors of the herbs.

Lower the oven temperature to 425°F (220°C, or gas mark 7). In a small saucepan, stir the Parmigiano-Reggiano cheese into the cream and mix well. Simmer gently over low heat until the cheese is melted and the sauce is fairly smooth (there will be a slight graininess to the sauce because of the texture of the cheese). Season with the nutmeg, black pepper, and a pinch of salt. Add the chives and stir. Cook the lasagna noodles according to the package directions. Drain the noodles and rinse them with cold water, then lay them out in one layer on a towel to dry.

[To assemble]
Lightly coat an 8" (20-cm) square baking dish with olive oil. Layer the bottom with pasta, and follow with a layer of asparagus and onion and a thin layer of grated Fontina and mozzarella cheese. Season lightly. Add another layer of pasta, and top with more asparagus, half of the Parmigiano cream sauce, and another thin layer of Fontina and mozzarella cheeses. Repeat until you use up the ingredients, ending with a layer of pasta. Pour the remaining Parmigiano cream on top, letting it run down the sides a bit.

Cover the dish with aluminum foil and bake for about 20 minutes. Remove the foil and continue to bake until the top is golden and bubbling, an additional 15 to 20 minutes. Remove from oven and let rest for 10 minutes before cutting.

[Variations]
Roasting vegetables concentrates and intensifies their flavors. Vegetables such as eggplant, butternut squash, leeks, peppers, tomatoes, and artichoke hearts are all great choices for roasting. Simply coat them in olive oil, toss with salt and black pepper, and roast in a hot oven until tender and brown. Layer in lasagna with a tomato-based sauce or with the Parmigiano cream sauce and cheeses in this recipe.
For an incredible variation in flavors, replace either the Fontina or mozzarella cheese with their smoked counterpart. Smoking cheese intensifies the flavors of the cheese, much as roasting vegetables does. In addition, it gives the cheese an earthy flavor of smoke.

[A note on fresh herbs]
Fresh herbs are like gold to any seasoned cook. The flavors and variations are endless. The contribution that fresh herbs make to any dish are irreplaceable. Unfortunately, fresh herbs are not always available, depending on the time of year and your location or available supermarkets. When you can find fresh herbs, they can be easily frozen for later use. Simply wash and clean the herbs thoroughly, being sure to pick any dead or rotting leaves from the bunch. Dry the herbs completely, layer on a paper towel in a single layer, and roll the paper towel from end to end tightly. Place them in an airtight container or freezer bag and freeze for later use. I do not suggest using frozen herbs in fresh sauces such as pesto, however; make the pesto when fresh herbs are available and freeze it.

In the case of basil and hard-stemmed, broad-leaved herbs, remove the leaves from the stems, freezing only the leaves of the plant.

[Substituting dried for fresh herbs]
In some cases, dried herbs are needed when fresh are not available. When using dried herbs, remember one simple rule: Use half as much of the dried as you would of the fresh. The flavors of dried herbs are concentrated and harsher than those of fresh, so less is needed.

[One herb for another]

Sometimes, when a recipe calls for one herb that is not available fresh, but dried is not preferred, there may be a fresh herb that can be substituted. For example, in the recipe for Roasted Asparagus Lasagna with Fontina Cheese, savory and tarragon are called for. In this case, if one or the other is not available, just increase the quantity of the one that is available to equal the quantity of the two. An herb like savory is similar in smell and flavor to oregano and marjoram. So, one of those could also be substituted if the other is not available. Generally, a recipe will tell you if dried can be used or if there is an alternative to the fresh one if it is not available. If that assistance is not in the recipe, then ask your local grocer.

Spring Vegetable Lasagna with Herbed Cream

When developing this recipe, I wanted to combine the garden-fresh flavors of greens with the crisp textures of spring vegetables. Instead of a typical ricotta cheese layer, I created a risotto-style filling with fresh herbs and goat cheese.

VEGETABLE FILLING

2 tablespoons (28 g) unsalted butter

2 tablespoons (28 ml) olive oil

2 cups (240 g) fresh zucchini, finely chopped

1 cup asparagus (100 g), trimmed, cut into 1-inch (2.5-cm) lengths

2 cups (200 g) fresh fennel bulbs, finely chopped

1 medium onion, finely chopped

1 cup (130 g) carrot, finely chopped

4 cloves garlic, minced

2 cups (200 g) shiitake mushrooms, thinly sliced

1 cup (100 g) radicchio, finely shredded

Salt and coarsely ground black pepper

16 ounces (455 g) fresh baby spinach

RISOTTO FILLING

1 tablespoon (14 g) unsalted butter

1 tablespoon (14 ml) olive oil

1 cup (195 g) Arborio rice

1 cup (235 ml) dry white wine

4 cups (950 ml) chicken or vegetable stock or canned broth

2 tablespoons (8 g) minced flat-leaf parsley

1/2 cup (50 g) freshly grated Parmigiano-Reggiano cheese

3 1/2 ounces (70 g) goat cheese

Salt and coarsely ground black pepper

HERBED CREAM

4 tablespoons (55 g) unsalted butter

4 tablespoons (3 g) all-purpose flour

1/2 cup (120 ml) dry white wine

2 cups (475 ml) chicken or vegetable stock or canned broth

3 tablespoons (7.5 g) fresh basil, minced

2 tablespoons (5 g) fresh tarragon, minced

3 tablespoons (7.5 g) fresh chives, minced

1 tablespoon (2 g) fennel tops, minced

1 teaspoon (5 g) orange zest, minced

1 cup (235 ml) heavy cream

Salt and coarsely ground black pepper

TO ASSEMBLE

12 sheets fresh or dried lasagna noodles

10 ounces (280 g) fresh mozzarella cheese, sliced thinly

Preheat oven to 400°F (200°C, or gas mark 6). Evenly coat a 9" × 13" (22.5 x 32.5 cm) baking dish with cooking spray or olive oil. In a large pot of salted, boiling water, cook the noodles, 10 minutes for dried or 2 to 3 minutes for fresh. Remove from water, rinse under cold water, drain, and set aside on paper towels to dry. For vegetable filling, melt 1 tablespoon (14 g) butter with 1 tablespoon (5 ml) olive oil in a large skillet over medium to high heat. Sauté zucchini, asparagus, fennel, onion, carrot, and garlic until tender and just beginning to color, about 15 minutes. Add shiitake mushrooms and radicchio. Combine and cook until wilted, about 3 minutes. Season with salt and pepper. Remove from heat and transfer to a platter. In the same skillet, heat the remaining tablespoon of butter and oil. Add the baby spinach, stirring to heat and wilt, about 2 minutes. Remove from heat and transfer to a platter.

[For risotto]
Melt butter with olive oil in a medium skillet over medium to high heat. Add the rice, coating it with butter and oil, stirring constantly to lightly brown, about 5 minutes. Add the wine and incorporate. Cook until all the wine has evaporated, about 5 minutes. Begin adding chicken stock to pan ½ cup (120 ml) at a time. Between additions of stock, cook until it has evaporated, stirring periodically to combine. The rice will begin to plump up and become tender. Continue this process of adding stock and cooking until all the stock has been used up. At this time, the risotto should have almost tripled in volume and be very fluffy and tender with a creamy consistency. If not, continue to add water or stock until a creamy consistency is reached. Remove from heat and transfer to a bowl. Add the parsley, Parmigiano-Reggiano, and goat cheese.

Stir to combine and melt cheeses. Add the salt and pepper to taste. Set aside to cool.

[For herbed cream]
Melt butter in a medium-sized saucepan over medium to high heat. Add flour and whisk to combine. Whisk continuously, cooking flour to a golden brown color. Combine the wine and stock together in a bowl. Gradually add the wine and stock mixture to the flour mixture, whisking constantly to combine. Add the liquid slowly to prevent lumps. Be careful of the steam that will rise from the pan at the initial addition of the liquid. After the addition of all the wine-stock mixture, add the basil, tarragon, chives, fennel tops, and orange zest. Stir to combine. Lower the heat to medium and continue to cook for about 2 minutes. Add the cream and simmer for 5 additional

minutes. Season with salt and pepper. Remove from the heat.

[To assemble lasagna]
Begin with 1 cup (235 ml) of herbed cream on the bottom of the baking dish. Top with three sheets of noodles, and layer with half of the spinach, then half of the vegetable mixture. Top the vegetables with 1 cup (235 ml) of herbed cream, and add one-third of the mozzarella cheese. Repeat with three pasta noodles. Add all of the risotto mixture in an even layer. If the risotto appears to be too dry after cooling, add about ¼ cup (60 ml) of heavy cream or milk to it to moisten it. Top the risotto with another layer of three noodles. Layer with remaining spinach, remaining vegetable mixture, about 1 cup (235 ml) of herbed cream, and one-third of the fresh mozzarella. Top with the last three noodles, then add the remaining herbed cream, finishing with the remaining mozzarella cheese. Bake uncovered for 30 minutes or until the top is bubbling and golden brown. Remove from the oven and let rest for 10 minutes before cutting to serve.

Grilled Vegetable Lasagna **with Fire-Roasted Red Pepper Sauce**

I love to grill vegetables no matter the occasion or time of year. While it is a bit more time-consuming, the taste is tremendous. There is no substitute for the intensity that fire imparts to the flavors of vegetables.

2 summer squash (approx. 1¼ pounds [570 g])

2 zucchini (approx. 1¼ pounds [570 g])

5 large carrots, peeled

¼ cup plus 2 tablespoons (90 ml) extra-virgin olive oil

1 tablespoon (6 g) black pepper

1 medium eggplant

2 portobello mushrooms, stems removed, wiped clean with a damp cloth

CHEESE FILLING

1 pound (500 g) ricotta cheese, whole milk or part skim

8 ounces (150 g) feta cheese, crumbled

½ cup (30 g) packed fresh basil leaves, sliced thinly

1 egg

1 pound (455 g) fresh or packaged dried lasagna noodles

1 recipe Fire-Roasted Red Pepper Sauce (recipe follows)

6 ounces (170 g) packaged baby spinach

8 ounces (112 g) shredded mozzarella cheese

FIRE-ROASTED RED PEPPER SAUCE

Makes approximately 3 cups (700 ml)

4 red peppers or 1 (16 ounce [450 g]) jar of roasted red peppers, drained

2 tablespoons (28 ml) extra-virgin olive oil

2 ¼ cups (500 ml) heavy cream

⅓ cup (75 g) freshly grated Parmesan cheese

Salt

½ teaspoon (1 g) black pepper

2 cloves garlic, crushed

2 tablespoons (5 g) fresh chopped basil leaves

[To prepare the vegetables]

Wash and clean all the vegetables, and slice the squash, zucchini, and carrots diagonally about ¼ inch (6 mm) thick. In a large bowl, toss the sliced squash, zucchini, and carrots with 2 tablespoons (28 ml) olive oil and 1 tablespoon (6 g) black pepper, coating it evenly. Set aside. Peel the eggplant and slice it into ¼-inch (6-mm) -thick rounds. Place the eggplant and the whole mushrooms on a plate and coat them evenly with the remaining ¼ cup (60 ml) of olive oil. On a hot outdoor grill or stove-top grill pan, grill the vegetables. Grill the squash, zucchini, carrots, and eggplant for about 7 minutes on each side; grill the mushrooms for about 20 minutes on each side. Grilling times will vary depending on the cooking surface and the appliance.

When grilling is complete, set all the vegetables aside for assembly, except the mushrooms. The mushrooms need to be sliced thin for assembly.

[To prepare the cheese filling]

In a large mixing bowl, combine the ricotta cheese, feta cheese, basil, and egg. Set aside.

[To assemble]

Preheat the oven to 350°F (180°C or gas mark 4). Oil the bottom and sides of a 9" × 13"

(22.5 cm × 32.5 cm) baking dish. If using store-bought dried noodles, prepare them according to package directions. If using fresh pasta, boil it in an ample amount of boiling, salted water for 2 to 3 minutes. Remove the noodles from the water and run them under cold water until cooled. Set aside on paper towels to dry. Using about ½ cup (125 g) red pepper sauce, evenly coat the bottom of the baking dish. Top the sauce with an even layer of lasagna noodles, being careful not to overlap them. Cut the lasagna noodles to fit the pan if necessary. Top the pasta with half of the baby spinach in an even layer, then with half of the vegetables, alternating the vegetables in an even layer. Top the vegetables with a sprinkling of half of the mozzarella cheese, then with another layer of lasagna noodles. Evenly coat the noodles with half of the ricotta cheese mixture. Top with another layer of lasagna noodles, then the remaining spinach, grilled vegetables, and mozzarella cheese. Add three additional lasagna noodles. Top the lasagna with the remaining red pepper sauce. Cover the pan and bake for 30 minutes. Uncover and bake an additional 15 to 20 minutes until the sauce is browned.

[Fire-Roasted Red Pepper Sauce]
Wash and dry the peppers thoroughly. Coat the red peppers with olive oil. On a hot grill, under the broiler of an electric oven, or over an open flame on a gas stove top, roast the peppers until the skin is charred black, turning them occasionally to ensure even roasting. When completely charred, place the peppers in a brown paper bag, sealing it for about 5 minutes. Remove peppers from the bag and remove the black skin. Cut peppers in half and remove the stems, seeds, and inner white veins. Chop peppers coarsely and set them aside.

In a heavy, medium-sized saucepan, heat the heavy cream. Add the grated Parmesan cheese, salt, and pepper to the cream and continue to heat it, stirring occasionally, until the cheese is melted and the sauce thickens. In the bowl of a food processor, combine the roasted red peppers and garlic, and purée. Add the pepper purée to the heavy cream mixture and combine. Heat through. Add the basil and stir. Remove from the heat and set aside until ready to use.

The sauce may be made ahead and refrigerated in an airtight container for up to three days or frozen for up to three months.

King Ranch Chicken Casserole

Back in my Camp Mystic kitchen days, this dish was a staple for lunch. Preparing it for 450 people was a bit more challenging and labor intensive than preparing it for your family or friends will be.

1 can (10.75 ounces [295 g]) cream of chicken soup

1 can (10.75 ounces [295 g]) cream of mushroom soup

2 cups (475 ml) chicken stock

1 can (10 ounces [280 g]) Ro-Tel brand tomatoes and green chiles

1 carton (10 ounces [280 g]) sliced mushrooms

1 teaspoon (3 g) chile powder

1/2 teaspoon (3 g) garlic salt

1/2 teaspoon (1 g) freshly cracked black pepper

12 corn tortillas, cut into triangles

1 chicken (1 3/4 pounds [785 g]), cooked and cut into bite-sized pieces

1 large yellow onion, chopped

1 cup (115 g) shredded American cheese

1 cup (115 g) shredded Monterey Jack cheese

Preheat oven to 350°F (180°C, or gas mark 4). Combine soups, chicken stock, tomatoes, mushrooms, chile powder, garlic salt and black pepper in a mixing bowl and set aside. Oil the bottom and sides of a 3-quart (2.8-L) casserole dish. Layer half of the tortilla pieces, half of the chicken, half of the chopped onion, and half of each cheese in the casserole dish. Pour half of chicken broth mixture over layers. Repeat layers of tortillas, chicken, and onion, and then pour remaining chicken broth over the top, finishing with remaining cheese. Bake for 45 to 60 minutes; serve hot. This dish may be frozen and reheated and will still taste great.

[serves 8]

Robust Tomato and Wild Mushroom Lasagna

Tomatoes and wild mushrooms come together in this hearty, wildly flavorful lasagna. With a bite of cayenne, the mushrooms' exotic tastes offer layers of rich, intense flavors throughout the dish.

2 tablespoons (28 ml) extra-virgin olive oil	2/3 cup (150 ml) dry white wine
1 large onion, minced	1 (28-ounce [825 ml]) can plus 1 (14-ounce [425 ml]) can crushed tomatoes in puree
3 ounces (55 g) prosciutto di Parma, finely chopped	1/4 teaspoon (1 g) paprika
1/2 cup (39 g) flat-leaf parsley, finely chopped	1/4 teaspoon (1 g) cayenne pepper
2 tablespoons (20 g) minced shallots	Salt and pepper
1 pound (455 g) assorted wild and exotic mushrooms (oyster, shiitake, lobster, cremini, etc.)	2 cups plus 2 tablespoons (210 g) grated Parmigiano-Reggiano cheese
2 cups (475 ml) beef broth	1 cup (150 g) grated mozzarella cheese plus 1/4 cup (38 g)
2 tablespoons (20 g) garlic, minced	1/2 cup (120 ml) heavy cream
3 tablespoons (7.5 g) fresh basil, chopped	1/4 cup (60 ml) milk
1 tablespoon (2.5 g) fresh oregano, chopped	1 pound (455 g) dried pasta sheets cooked according to package directions, or 1 pound (455 g) fresh pasta blanched for 2 minutes and drained

Preheat the oven to 350°F (180°C, or gas mark 4). Lightly oil a 9" × 13" (22.5 x 32.5 cm) baking dish.

In a large sauté pan, heat the olive oil. When the oil is hot, sauté the onions and prosciutto for about 3 minutes or until the onions are wilted and begin to caramelize.

Add 1/2 cup (30 g) of minced parsley, shallots, and mushrooms. Combine and sauté for about 5 minutes or until the mushrooms begin to brown and soften. Add 2 cups (475 ml) of beef broth, stirring vigorously to deglaze the pan—continue to cook for an additional 45 minutes to concentrate the flavors. Season with salt and pepper. Stir in the garlic, basil, and oregano. Cook for an additional 3 minutes. Remove the mixture from the heat. Strain the mushroom mixture, reserving the liquid.

Pour the liquid back into the sauté pan. Heat and stir vigorously to remove any particles along the sides of the pan. Add the wine and continue to deglaze the pan. Continue to cook the liquid until a glaze is formed, about 15 minutes, stirring occasionally. Add the tomatoes, paprika, and cayenne, and combine thoroughly. Continue to cook for 20 minutes, stirring occasionally. Season with salt and pepper. Add the mushroom mixture to the sauce. Combine and remove the sauce from the heat.

[To assemble]

Spoon a small amount of the sauce on the bottom of the baking dish, covering evenly. Layer pasta sheets over the sauce, being careful not to overlap them. Cut the pasta sheets to fit the baking dish if necessary. Repeat with a thick layer of mushroom sauce. Sprinkle with Parmigiano-Reggiano and a generous amount of mozzarella cheese. Top with three additional sheets of pasta and repeat with remaining mushroom sauce, Parmesan cheese, mozzarella cheese, and pasta sheets. Ensure the last layer in the baking dish is the pasta. Mix ½ cup (120 ml) heavy cream with ¼ cup (60 ml) milk, 2 tablespoons (10 g) Parmigiano-Reggiano cheese, and ¼ cup (40 g) mozzarella cheese. Season with salt and pepper. Pour over the top of the lasagna. Cover the lasagna with foil and bake for 30 minutes. Remove the cover and bake for an additional 15 to 20 minutes or until the top layer of cheese becomes brown and bubbly. Remove from oven. Allow to rest for 10 minutes before cutting to serve. If there is any remaining mushroom sauce, serve alongside the lasagna.

[serves 9]

Italian Grinder Lasagna

Sitting in a little Italian pizzeria one day,
I ordered the meaty stuffed pizza. One bite into
it and I thought, "This has to be a lasagna."
I love the dense texture of this dish—I believe
you will, too.

1 pound (455 g) ricotta cheese

3 tablespoons (7.5 g) fresh basil, chopped

1 tablespoon (4 g) dried oregano

2 eggs

1/8 teaspoon (.25 g) red pepper flakes

1/4 cup (25 g) grated Parmesan cheese

1 pound (455 g) dried lasagna noodles or fresh pasta sheets cut into lasagna noodles

2 1/4 cups (535 ml) Quick Tomato Sauce (see page 65)

1/2 pound (225 g) prosciutto, thinly sliced

1/2 pound (225 g) Genoa salami, thinly sliced

1/2 pound (225 g) smoked deli ham, thinly sliced

1/2 pound (225 g) sweet capicola, thinly sliced

1/2 pound (225 g) provolone cheese, thinly sliced

1/2 pound (225 g) shredded mozzarella cheese

Preheat oven to 375°F (109°C, or gas mark 5). Coat the bottom and sides of a 9" ×13" (22.5 x 32.5 cm) baking dish evenly with olive oil. In a large mixing bowl, combine ricotta cheese, basil, oregano, eggs, pepper flakes, and Parmesan cheese. Mix until eggs are thoroughly combined.

In a large pot of salted, boiling water, cook the dried pasta according to package directions; alternatively, cook fresh pasta for 2 minutes. Drain the pasta and rinse it with cold water. Place it on a paper towel to dry before using it in the dish.

Place 3/4 cup (175 ml) tomato sauce on the bottom of the baking dish. Top with a layer of lasagna noodles. Top noodles with 1/3 cup (65 g) of the ricotta cheese mixture, spreading evenly over the noodles. Top with another layer of pasta. Top pasta with half of the meats, layering them evenly. Top the meat with half of the provolone, and top this with half of the shredded mozzarella cheese. Repeat with a layer of pasta, then 3/4 cup (175 g) of sauce, then 1/3 (65 g) cup ricotta cheese mixture. Top the ricotta cheese mixture with another layer of pasta, then the remainder of the meats, provolone cheese, and mozzarella cheese. Finish with a final layer of pasta, topped with the remainder of the tomato sauce and randomly placed dollops of the remaining ricotta cheese mixture.

Coat a large sheet of aluminum foil with oil and cover the baking pan with it, oil-side down. Bake for 30 minutes, covered. Remove foil and bake for an additional 15 to 20 minutes or until the top is bubbly and the cheese begins to brown. Remove the lasagna from the oven and let it rest for 10 minutes before cutting to serve.

Four-Cheese Lasagna

Varying the tomato sauce will alter the flavor from deep and rich to fresh and springlike. Whatever your decision, the cheeses will pair perfectly and the flavors will be simple but elegant.

2 tablespoons (28 ml) vegetable or olive oil

1 (16-ounce [455 g]) package dry lasagna noodles or 1 pound fresh noodles

1 recipe Quick Tomato Sauce (recipe follows)

2 pounds (1 kg) ricotta or cottage cheese

1/2 cup (30 g) chopped fresh basil

1/2 cup (30 g) chopped fresh parsley

8 ounces (75 g) shredded mozzarella cheese

8 ounces (75 g) crumbled feta cheese

1 cup (100 g) grated Parmesan cheese

QUICK TOMATO SAUCE

Makes 4 cups (1 L)

3 1/2 pounds (1 1/2 kg) canned best-quality, peeled plum tomatoes with juice

4 cloves garlic, peeled and coarsely chopped

1 tablespoon (18 g) coarse salt

1 tablespoon (15 g) sugar

6 tablespoons (84 ml) extra-virgin olive oil

1 1/4 cup (50 g) loosely packed fresh basil leaves

2 tablespoons (30 g) tomato paste

1/4 teaspoon (5 mg) black pepper

2 teaspoons (3 g) dried oregano

1/4 cup (50 ml) red wine

Preheat oven to 375°F (190°C, or gas mark 5). Oil the sides and bottom of a 9" × 13" (22.5 x 32.5 cm) baking dish. Bring a large pot of lightly salted water to a boil. Add dried pasta and cook for 8 to 10 minutes, or until al dente. If using fresh pasta, cook for only 2 to 4 minutes. Drain pasta and rinse under cold water. Set aside.

In a blender or with an electric mixer, blend the tomato sauce and ricotta cheese together until smooth. In a small bowl, combine the basil and parsley. Spoon about 1/2 cup (125 ml) of the sauce mixture into the bottom of the baking dish, covering completely. Add a layer of cooked pasta over the sauce,

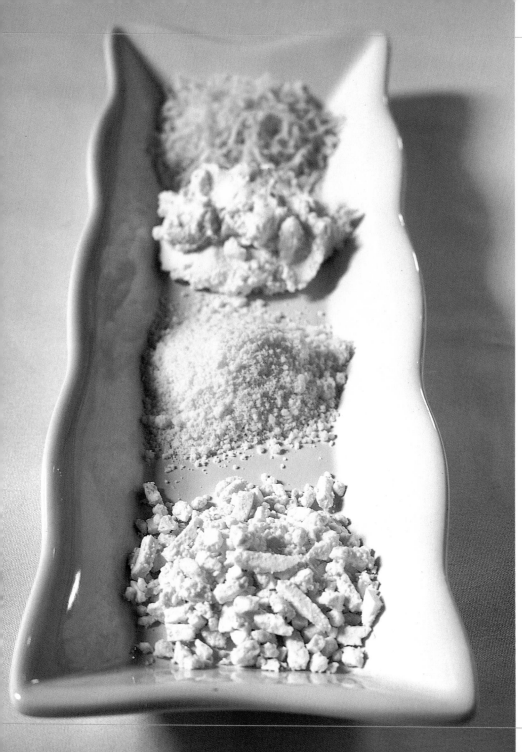

and sprinkle one-third of each of the mozzarella, feta, Parmesan, and herbs over the noodles. Repeat the layering one-third of each of the sauce, noodles, cheeses, and herbs, finishing with remaining cheeses and herbs.

Bake for 30 to 45 minutes until the cheese is bubbly and golden. Remove from the oven and let rest for 10 minutes before slicing to serve.

[For Quick Tomato Sauce]
Place all the ingredients in a large saucepan. Bring to a boil, stirring and boiling for about 5 minutes, crushing the tomatoes with the back of a spoon while stirring. Reduce the heat and simmer for 20 minutes, stirring occasionally. Serve immediately or refrigerate for up to five days. The sauce may be made, chilled, and frozen in airtight containers for up to three months.

1 pound (455 g) fresh or 4 dried lasagna noodles

1 recipe Bolognese Meat Sauce (see page 46)

1 recipe Béchamel Sauce (recipe follows)

1/2 pound (225 g) Italian Fontina cheese cut into strips

BÉCHAMEL SAUCE

Makes about 2 cups (475 ml)

3 tablespoons (45 g) unsalted butter

3 tablespoons (24 g) flour

1 cup (235 ml) dry white wine

1 cup (235 ml) whole milk

1 tablespoon (15 g) Dijon mustard

1/4 teaspoon (5 mg) nutmeg

Salt

White pepper

[serves 9]

Lasagna **Bolognese**

Here, feather-light lasagna noodles surround rich layers of hearty meat sauce and creamy béchamel, giving way to timeless tradition. Typically, Lasagna Bolognese would be made with homemade "green" or spinach pasta sheets. Either fresh or store-bought pasta can be used here.

Preheat oven to 350°F (180°C, or gas mark 4). Bring a large pot of salted water to a boil. Cook dried pasta for 8 to 10 minutes, until al dente. Cook fresh pasta for 2 to 3 minutes. Drain pasta, toss with 1 tablespoon (15 ml) olive oil and set aside. In an oiled 13"× 9"(22.5 x 32.5 cm) baking dish, place a layer of drained noodles, just barely overlapping. Cover with about one-third of the meat sauce and then one-third of the béchamel sauce. Top with about one-quarter of the Fontina cheese strips. Repeat layers two more times. Finish with a layer of noodles followed by the remaining cheese strips. Bake uncovered for 45 minutes or until top is golden and bubbly. Remove from oven and let stand for 10 minutes before cutting into squares to serve.

[For Béchamel Sauce]
Scald the milk in a medium-sized saucepan over medium heat, stirring occasionally, until bubbles form around the sides, then turn off the heat. Melt the butter in a medium-sized skillet over medium-high heat. Add flour to butter, whisking thoroughly to combine. Cook until just turning tan in color, stirring constantly, about 3 minutes. Once roux has reached a light tan color, reduce heat to low, add the white wine, and stir vigorously to incorporate without leaving lumps. Once sauce is thick, gradually add scalded milk, 1/3 cup (75 ml) at a time, stirring vigorously and continuously between additions to prevent lumps. Add Dijon mustard and nutmeg and season with salt and pepper. The sauce is done when it coats the back of a wooden spoon. If it appears too thick, add more milk.

Triple-Cheese Baked Chicken and Macaroni

Macaroni and cheese is a traditional comfort food. I decided to pump up a classic, making it a meal in and of itself, with chicken and mushrooms.

3/4 pound (340 g) elbow macaroni

1 tablespoon (15 ml) olive oil

7 tablespoons (100 g) unsalted butter, divided

1 small white onion, chopped

1/2 cup (40 g) sliced baby bella or cremini mushrooms

1 package (10 ounces [280 g]) frozen green peas, thawed

1/2 cup (30 g) all-purpose flour

1 teaspoon (3 g) dried mustard

1/2 teaspoon (1.5 g) ancho chile powder

2 cups (475 ml) milk, heated with 2 whole cloves and 1 bay leaf

1/2 cup (120 ml) heavy cream

2/3 pound (300 g) cooked chicken breast, shredded

3 tablespoons (9 g) chopped fresh chives

2 teaspoons (10 ml) dry sherry

1/2 cup (55 g) finely shredded Fontina cheese

1/2 cup (55 g) finely shredded smoked Gruyère cheese

1/2 cup plus 3 tablespoons (85 g) shredded white Cheddar cheese

1 cup (115 g) fine dried bread crumbs

Preheat oven to 350°F (180°C, or gas mark 4). Boil the macaroni in a large pot of salted water until al dente, about 10 minutes, drain, toss with 1 tablespoon (15 ml) olive oil, and set aside. In the same large pot, melt 4 tablespoons (55 g) butter over medium-high heat, add the onion, and sauté until tender, about 4 minutes. Add the mushrooms and sauté until tender, about 4 minutes; add the peas and heat through, sprinkle with flour, mustard, and chile powder; cook 2 minutes to brown the flour a bit. Remove the cloves and bay leaf from the milk and discard. Add the warm milk to the flour mixture 1 cup (235 ml) at a time, stirring vigorously during each addition. Add the heavy cream, bring to a boil, and reduce heat to a simmer.

Add the chicken, chives, and sherry, cooking for 3 minutes. Add Fontina, Gruyère, and ½ cup (60 g) Cheddar cheese; stir to melt and combine. Add cooked macaroni and stir to combine. Remove from heat and pour into a greased 3-quart (2.8-L) baking dish, topping with remaining shredded Cheddar cheese. In a small skillet, melt remaining 3 tablespoons (45 g) butter over medium heat; add bread crumbs, tossing to coat evenly with butter. Cook for 3 minutes, stirring constantly to toast bread crumbs. Remove from heat, sprinkle over macaroni dish. Place dish on middle rack of oven and bake for 45 minutes to 1 hour, until bubbling and browned on top. Remove, let rest for 10 minutes, serve hot.

Broccoli Lasagna with Mushrooms and Fontina Cheese

In this easy-to-prepare dish, the robust flavor of Fontina cheese lends itself well to the crunch of broccoli and the exotic flavors of mushrooms.

9 lasagna noodles, dried or fresh

1 tablespoon (14 g) unsalted butter

2 tablespoons (28 ml) olive oil

2 shallots, chopped

3 cloves garlic, minced

1 medium carrot, chopped

1 medium parsnip, chopped

10 ounces (280 g) mushrooms (such as Bella or crimini), sliced thin

2 (10-ounce [285 ml]) packages frozen broccoli, thawed and chopped

1 tablespoon (4 g) fresh flat-leaf parsley, minced

Salt and coarsly ground black pepper

1 recipe Béchamel Sauce, increased by half (see page 67)

1/2 cup (120 ml) milk

1 pound (455 g) Fontina cheese, shredded

Zest of one lemon

Pinch of grated nutmeg

2 tablespoons (5 g) fresh basil, chopped

1 cup (100 g) grated Parmesan cheese

9 ounces (255 g) goat cheese (such as Montrachet)

Preheat oven to 400ºF (200ºC, or gas mark 6). Coat insides of a 13"× 9"(22.5 x 32.5 cm) baking dish with cooking spray or olive oil. In a large pot of boiling, salted water, cook the lasagna noodles until al dente, 10 minutes for dried, 2 to 3 minutes for fresh. Remove noodles from water, rinse under cold water, and set aside on a towel to dry.

Melt the butter with the olive oil in a large sauté pan over medium to high heat. Sauté the shallots with the garlic, carrot, and parsnip until the shallots begin to brown and the carrots and parsnips become tender, about 5 minutes. Add the mushrooms and continue to cook, allowing the mushrooms to sweat and wilt, about 4 minutes. Add the broccoli and parsley, stirring to combine. Continue to cook for an additional 2 minutes to heat broccoli through. Season with salt and pepper, remove from heat, and set aside. In a medium-sized saucepan, heat the béchamel sauce. Add ½ cup (120 ml) milk to thin, bring to a simmer, add Fontina cheese and lemon zest, and cook over medium heat, stirring constantly until smooth and creamy and Fontina cheese is melted, about 15 minutes. Season with nutmeg and salt and pepper.

[To assemble]
In the baking dish, layer 1 cup (235 ml) of the Fontina cheese sauce, three lasagna noodles, 1 cup (235 ml) more Fontina cheese sauce, half the broccoli-mushroom mixture, half the chopped basil, one-third of the Parmesan cheese, and one-third of the goat cheese. Top with three additional noodles, half of the remaining Fontina cheese sauce, remaining broccoli-mushroom mixture, remaining basil, one-third of the Parmesan cheese, and one-third of the goat cheese. Top with remaining three noodles and Fontina cheese sauce, then sprinkle with the remaining Parmesan and goat cheese. Cover with foil coated with cooking spray. Bake for 20 minutes, uncover, and bake for an additional 10 to 15 minutes until top is golden and bubbly. Remove from oven and let rest for 10 minutes before cutting to serve.

3 pounds (1.4 kg) portobello mushrooms, sliced

1 large onion, peeled, cut in half, and sliced thinly

3 cloves garlic, minced

1/4 cup (15 g) fresh basil, thinly sliced

2 tablespoons (5 g) flat-leaf parsley, minced

4 tablespoons (55 ml) extra-virgin olive oil

2 tablespoons (28 g) unsalted butter, cut into chunks

1 cup (235 ml) chicken broth

1/2 teaspoon (1 g) cayenne pepper

1/2 teaspoon (1 g) ground coriander

8 ounces (112 g) Asiago cheese, shredded

8 ounces (112 g) mozzarella cheese, shredded

2 cups (475 ml) Quick Tomato Sauce (see page 65)

6 ounces (15 g) fresh arugula

1 pound (455 g) fresh or dried lasagna noodles

Roasted Portobello and Caramelized Onion Lasagna

This is a light dish with the robust, flavors of roasted portobello mushrooms. The only cheeses in this dish are the shredded Asiago and mozzarella. There is no heavy layer of ricotta or creamy sauce, just fresh mushrooms and arugula.

Preheat oven to 400°F (200°C, or gas mark 6). Bring a large pot of salted water to a boil. Cook dried pasta for 8 to 10 minutes, until al dente. (Cook fresh pasta for 2 to 3 minutes.) Drain noodles, rinse under cold water, and set aside on a kitchen towel or paper towel to dry. Combine the mushrooms, onion, garlic, basil, and parsley in a large baking dish. Drizzle with olive oil, tossing with your hands to coat evenly. Top with chunks of butter. Pour the chicken broth over the vegetables, then add the cayenne pepper and coriander.

Place in the oven and cook, uncovered, until the vegetables are tender and beginning to brown, about 20 to 30 minutes. Remove from the heat and set aside. In a large mixing bowl, combine the Asiago and mozzarella cheese and set it aside.

[To assemble]

In a well-oiled 9" × 13" (22.5 x 32.5 cm) baking dish, place 1 cup of tomato sauce on the bottom. Top with three lasagna noodles, and place half of the mushroom mixture on top of the noodles, topping with half of the arugula

and then with about one third of the shredded cheeses. Top the cheeses with pasta noodles, add 1½ cups (355 ml) sauce, and repeat the layers with the remaining mushroom mixture, one third of the cheeses, and the remaining arugula. Add the remaining three lasagna noodles, and top with the remaining tomato sauce and cheeses. Place in the oven and bake until bubbly and golden, about 45 minutes. Remove from oven and let cool for 10 minutes prior to serving.

Potato Gratin Lasagna

This is an adaptation of a great vegetable side dish. The lasagna noodles give it more layers and a firm consistency. Cut it into smaller portions and serve it as a side with roasted chicken. Larger portions served with a salad make a great vegetarian meal.

2 tablespoons (28 ml) olive oil

1 medium yellow onion, thinly sliced

2 tablespoons (20 g) garlic, minced

10 Roma tomatoes (1¹/₂ pounds [570 g]), seeded, cut into chunks

2 teaspoons (1.5 g) fresh rosemary, minced

1 teaspoon (.8 g) fresh oregano, minced

2 tablespoons (5 g) fresh basil, minced

1 tablespoon (14 g) butter

¹/₂ cup (55 g) toasted bread crumbs

6 dried or fresh lasagna noodles

4 russet potatoes, peeled and thinly sliced

Salt and pepper

1 cup (120 g) grated Swiss cheese

1 cup (120 g) grated Gruyère cheese

Preheat oven to 450°F (230°C, or gas mark 8). Spray a 9" × 13" (22.5 × 32.5 cm) baking dish with cooking spray. Bring a large pot of salted water to a boil. Cook dried pasta for 8 to 10 minutes, until al dente. (Cook fresh pasta for 2 to 3 minutes.) Drain noodles, rinse under cold water, and set aside on a kitchen towel or paper towel to dry. Sauté the onions in a skillet over medium-high heat with olive oil until just soft. Stir in the garlic, and cook another minute until just aromatic. Add tomatoes, rosemary, oregano, and basil. Continue to cook until all moisture has evaporated, about 10 minutes.

[Toasting bread crumbs]
In a skillet (preferably Teflon-coated), melt 1 tablespoon (14 g) butter. Add the bread crumbs and combine, stirring to coat evenly while cooking. Cook until golden brown and aromatic, about 5 minutes. Remove from the heat and allow to cool.

[To assemble]
Layer one-third of the lasagna noodles in the prepared casserole dish. Top with half of the sliced potatoes, and season with salt and pepper. Top the potatoes with half of the tomato mixture, and sprinkle with half the grated cheeses. Repeat the layering, ending with cheese. Sprinkle evenly with toasted bread crumbs. Cover the gratin with foil and bake for 30 minutes. Remove the foil and bake for an additional 15 to 20 minutes to brown the cheese. Let stand 5 minutes to set the cheese before slicing and serving.

12 dried or fresh lasagna noodles

2 tablespoons (28 ml) olive oil

1 cup (130 g) onion, chopped

1 cup (100 g) shiitake mushrooms, stems removed, finely chopped

1 clove garlic, finely minced

8 ounces (115 g) cream cheese

1 1/2 cups (335 g) cottage cheese

1/2 cup (55 g) shredded mozzarella cheese

1 egg

1 tablespoon (2.5 g) chopped fresh basil or 2 teaspoons (8 g) dried

1/4 teaspoon (2 g) salt

1/4 teaspoon (.5 g) black pepper

1 pound (455 g) cooked baby shrimp, chopped

7 ounces (200 g) lump crabmeat, cleaned of any shells, chopped

2 cups (475 ml) condensed mushroom soup

1/3 cup (150 ml) milk

1/3 cup (150 ml) dry white wine

1/4 cup (25 g) grated Parmesan cheese

Fresh basil leaves for garnish

Seafood Lasagna **Roulades**

This is a tremendous dish with intense flavors and a very elegant presentation. The roulades are a simple way to use lasagna noodles with beautiful results. Serve these with fresh steamed or roasted asparagus spears.

Bring a large pot of salted water to a boil. Cook dried pasta for 8 to 10 minutes, until al dente. (Cook fresh pasta for 2 to 3 minutes.) Drain noodles, rinse under cold water, and set aside on a kitchen towel or paper towel to dry. Heat the olive oil in a large skillet over medium-high heat. Add the onion, mushrooms, and garlic and sauté until they are tender and the mushrooms begin to give off their juices and darken, about 7 minutes. Transfer the onion and mushroom mixture in a mixing bowl and add the cream cheese. Gradually stir in the cottage cheese, mozzarella cheese, egg, basil, salt, and pepper. Add the shrimp and crab to the mixture; combine well. In another mixing bowl, combine mushroom soup, milk, and wine. Oil a 9" × 13" (22.5 × 32.5 cm) baking dish and coat the bottom with half of the mushroom mixture. To assemble roulades, lay the lasagna noodles flat on a large work surface, and spread the seafood mixture evenly over the lasagna noodles, staying close to the edge of the pasta. Begin at one end and roll the noodle up into a cylinder. Place it seam-side down in the baking dish. Repeat with remainder of the noodles and filling. Top roulades with remainder of mushroom sauce and Parmesan cheese. Bake at 350°F (180°C, or gas mark 4) for 20 to 30 minutes until the tops are bubbling and begin to brown. Remove roulades from oven and let them rest for 5 minutes before serving. Serve two roulades per person, garnishing them with fresh basil leaves and sauce from the bottom of the baking dish.

Baked Pasta **Primavera** with Broccolini and Fennel

Pasta primavera is a great choice for vegetarian diets. Although sometimes mundane, this baked version benefits from the zest of three cheeses and a combination of vegetables and mushrooms.

1 box (16 ounces [455 g]) ziti pasta

2 containers (10 ounces [280 g] each) prepared Alfredo sauce

1 container (8 ounces [225 g]) sour cream

1/4 cup (25 g) grated Parmesan cheese

2 cups (230 g) shredded mozzarella cheese

1/4 cup (15 g) chopped fresh flat-leaf parsley

2 tablespoons (6 g) fresh chopped chives

3 tablespoons (45 ml) olive oil

2 cups (140 g) sliced shiitake mushrooms

2 small bulbs fennel, cleaned, sliced very thin

3 cloves fresh garlic, minced

Salt and pepper

1 tablespoon (2 g) chopped fresh fennel leaves

1 package (6 ounces [170 g]) broccolini spears, blanched

1 1/2 pounds (680 g) asparagus spears, blanched, chopped

1 package (6 ounces [170 g]) shredded carrots

1 package (8 ounces [225 g]) frozen sugar snap peas, defrosted

1 red bell pepper, sliced thin

1 yellow bell pepper, sliced thin

Prepare ziti according to package directions; drain and return to pot. In a large mixing bowl, stir together Alfredo sauce, sour cream, Parmesan cheese, 1 cup (115 g) mozzarella cheese, parsley, and chives. Add Alfredo sauce mixture to pasta and stir to combine. In a large skillet, heat olive oil over medium-high heat, add mushrooms and fennel, sautéing until tender, about 5 minutes. Add garlic to skillet and sauté for an additional 3 minutes. Season with salt and black pepper, add chopped fennel leaves, and stir to combine. To the pasta mixture, add sautéed mushroom mixture, blanched broccolini and asparagus, carrots, peas, red and yellow peppers; stir to combine all. Transfer pasta mixture into a

9" × 13" (22.5 x 32.5 cm) baking dish with 3" (7.5-cm) sides. Top with remaining 1 cup (115 g) shredded mozzarella cheese, wrap tightly with plastic wrap, and refrigerate for up to 5 days. If you wish to freeze for a later date, wrap tightly with plastic wrap and heavy-duty aluminum foil. May be frozen for up to one month. To prepare for service, remove from refrigerator and let stand for 10 minutes, remove plastic wrap, and place in a 375°F (190°C, or gas mark 5) oven and bake for 45 minutes. If preparing for service from a frozen state, transfer to refrigerator and thaw for 24 hours. Remove plastic wrap and foil, place in 375°F (190°C, or gas mark 5) oven, and bake for 45 minutes. Remove and serve warm.

[Cook's Note]

How to Blanch Vegetables

Bring a large pot of salted water to a rolling boil. Prepare a large, deep bowl full of ice and water. Add raw vegetables to boiling water and blanch for 30 seconds to 3 minutes, depending on desired degree of doneness and the size of the vegetable being blanched. After the 30 seconds to 3 minutes of cooking time, remove vegetable from boiling water using a slotted spoon and plunge into the ice-water bath to "shock" the vegetables. Once chilled completely, remove and allow to drain, patting dry. At this time, vegetables are ready for use. Typically, the purpose of blanching is to make raw vegetables tender for either raw consumption (like crudités) or for additional cooking, as in the case of the Baked Pasta Primavera.

1 pound (455 g) rigatoni

2 tablespoons (28 ml) olive oil, plus more as needed

1 yellow onion, chopped

2 garlic cloves, chopped

1 pound (455 g) ground hot Italian sausage or chorizo

1 bunch kale, tough stems removed, chopped

1/2 cup (30 g) chopped fresh flat-leaf parsley

1 tablespoon (4 g) dried oregano

1 tablespoon (2.5 g) fresh basil, chopped

2 cans (14.5 ounces [411 g] each) fire-roasted diced tomatoes (available in specialty gourmet markets) or 1 large can (28 ounces [785 g]) peeled and chopped tomatoes

1 cup (235 ml) heavy cream

Salt and freshly ground pepper

8 (2" [5-cm]) fully cooked meatballs, chopped (recipe is on page 82)

1/2 pound (225 g) whole-milk mozzarella cheese, shredded

1/2 cup (50 g) grated Parmesan cheese

1/2 cup (60 g) grated smoked Gruyère or provolone cheese

Baked Rigatoni **with Meatballs, Sausage, and Kale**

This hearty, dish piles up layers of flavors, with incredible meatballs, ground sausage, and kale. A bit of a Portuguese influence comes from the sausage and kale, but it is true Italian comfort food, with layers of cheese and pasta blanketing the meats.

Preheat an oven to 350°F (180°C, or gas mark 4).

Cook rigatoni in a large pot of salted boiling water, stirring well, until al dente, about 12 minutes or according to the package instructions. Drain the rigatoni, place in a large bowl, and toss with a little olive oil to prevent sticking. Set aside.

In the same pot, heat the 2 tablespoons (28 ml) olive oil over medium-high heat. Add the onion and garlic and cook, stirring, until tender, about 5 minutes. Add the sausage and cook until no red remains, about 15 minutes. Add the kale and sauté, stirring, until wilted, about 3 additional minutes. Add the parsley, oregano, basil, and tomatoes and stir well. Bring to a boil, and then reduce the heat to low and simmer, uncovered, for 20 minutes. Stir in the cream, increase the heat, and return to a boil. Remove from the heat and season with salt and pepper. Return the rigatoni to the pot with the sauce, add the meatballs, and toss to coat well.

Oil the bottom of a shallow 3-quart (2.8-L) baking dish. Add half of the pasta mixture, spreading evenly in the bottom of the dish. Sprinkle with half of the mozzarella. Top with the remaining pasta, then the remaining mozzarella, followed by the Parmesan and Gruyère cheese. Bake until the sauce is bubbly and the top is golden brown, about 35 minutes. Remove from the oven, let stand for about 5 minutes, and serve.

Mama Rose's Meatball Lasagna

I think the only lasagna recipe that is more traditional than this is lasagna Bolognese. Meatball lasagna has been around for years. To find the perfect recipe, I relied on a well-versed Italian to lead me in the right direction. Rose's lasagna recipe is absolutely delicious.

12 dried lasagna noodles

MEATBALLS

2 pounds (1 kg) ground beef

2 cloves fresh garlic, minced

1/4 cup (30 g) seasoned bread crumbs

1/4 cup (25 g) grated Romano cheese

2 eggs

1/2 teaspoon (3 g) salt

1/2 teaspoon (1 g) coarsely ground black pepper

Vegetable oil for frying

TOMATO SAUCE

2 (28-ounce [825 ml]) cans whole peeled plum tomatoes

1 cup (60 g) fresh basil

1/2 cup (120 ml) tomato sauce

2 tablespoons (36 g) seasoning salt

1 (6-ounce [175 ml]) can tomato paste with garlic

1/4 teaspoon (.5 g) coarse ground black pepper

CHEESE FILLING

2 pounds (1 kg) ricotta cheese

3/4 cup (75 g) Romano cheese

Preheat oven to 400°F (200°C, or gas mark 6). Evenly coat a 9" × 13" (22.5 × 32.5 cm) baking dish with cooking spray or olive oil. In a large pot of boiling, salted water, cook the lasagna noodles to al dente for 10 minutes. Drain the noodles and return to the pot. Fill pot with cold water and leave noodles until you're ready to use them. Once ready for assembly, remove one noodle at a time, pat it dry, and place it in the baking dish.

[For meatballs]
In large mixing bowl, combine all ingredients. Using your hands, crush the ingredients together until smooth. If needed, add cold water to achieve a moist, yet firm consistency. To form meatballs, moisten hands with cold water and roll mounds of the mixture (the size of golf balls) together to form balls. Moisten your hands with cold tap water between each meatball to prevent sticking. Place meatballs on a platter and set aside.

[For tomato sauce]
Combine all ingredients in a medium stockpot. Bring to a boil, stirring to incorporate, reduce heat to a simmer, and allow to simmer while finishing meatball preparation.
Fill a large skillet with vegetable or canola oil 1" (2.5 cm) up the sides. Heat oil over medium to high heat. Once oil is hot, fry the meatballs until brown on all sides, about 5 minutes. Remove the meatballs from oil and place on a paper towel to drain for a minute or two. Add meatballs to tomato sauce and let cook for 5 minutes.

[For cheese filling]
In a medium mixing bowl, combine cheeses, stirring thoroughly to combine to a creamy consistency.

[To assemble]
Remove meatballs from tomato sauce and place in a bowl. Using a fork or potato masher, crush meatballs into a crumbly consistency and set aside. In a baking dish, place 1 cup (235 ml) of tomato sauce, layer four lasagna noodles, overlapping each other, over the sauce. Top noodles with crushed meatballs, then add 1 cup (235 ml) of tomato sauce. Top with four more lasagna noodles overlapping each other, then add ricotta cheese mixture. Layer remaining lasagna noodles, making sure that they overlap each other. Top with remaining sauce. Cover the lasagna with aluminum foil and bake for 30 minutes, until bubbling. Remove from oven and let rest for 10 minutes before serving.

Perfect One-Dish Meals

Pesto Lasagna with Roasted Red and Yellow Peppers

This is a great take on the traditional Lasagna con Pesto from the Ligurian region of Italy. A bright summer day and a silky glass of Pinot Grigio are the best accompaniments for this dish.

12 sheets dried lasagna noodles

1 cup (250 g) ricotta cheese

4 ounces (115 g) goat cheese

8 ounces (225 g) Fontina cheese, shredded

8 ounces (225 g) mozzarella cheese, shredded

4 cups (1 L) basil pesto

6 ounces (170 g) roasted red bell peppers, drained and thinly sliced

6 ounces (170 g) roasted yellow bell peppers, drained and thinly sliced

Olive oil

Preheat oven to 375°F (109°C, or gas maark 5). Oil bottom and sides of an 8" × 8" (20-cm) baking dish. Bring a large pot of salted water to a boil. Boil pasta noodles for 10 minutes until al dente. Drain noodles and toss with olive oil, set aside.

In a small bowl, combine the ricotta and goat cheeses, and blend well. In another small bowl, combine the Fontina and mozzarella cheeses. Line the bottom of the baking dish with three sheets of cooked pasta, and top with one-third of the pesto and one-third of the Fontina cheese mixture. Add another layer of three pasta sheets.

Top with half of the ricotta cheese mixture and then with two-thirds of the roasted red and yellow peppers, followed by one third of the Fontina cheese mixture. Then add three more sheets of pasta. Repeat with a layer of pesto, then the remaining Fontina cheese mixture, three pasta sheets, ricotta cheese mixture, roasted peppers, and the pesto as the last layer.

Bake for 30 minutes until bubbly and the pesto begins to darken around the edges. Remove from oven and let rest 10 minutes before cutting to serve. For an easier, thinner dish, omit the ricotta cheese mixture from the layers. The result is less rich and a bit oilier, but still tastes terrific.

Buffalo Chicken Lasagna

A great Super Bowl Sunday dish, without all the napkins. You can eat this buffalo chicken with a fork rather than your hands and still have all the great, spicy flavors of your favorite hot wings. If you want, dip some fresh celery sticks into the sauce.

9 dried lasagna noodles

1 tablespoon (14 g) butter

2 tablespoons (28 ml) extra-virgin olive oil

1 small onion, chopped

3 cloves garlic, minced

1 small green bell pepper, chopped

1 small red bell pepper, chopped

1 pound (455 g) skinless, boneless chicken breasts, cooked and diced

1/2 teaspoon (.5 g) cayenne pepper

2 tablespoons (28 ml) apple cider vinegar

2 tablespoons (28 ml) Worcestershire sauce

1 tablespoon (15 g) Thai curry paste, optional

1 recipe Quick Tomato Sauce (see page 65)

1 1/2 cups (355 ml) water

3 tablespoons (45 ml) hot sauce

1 egg, beaten

1 (15-ounce [420 g]) container ricotta cheese

2 cups (66 g) shredded mozzarella cheese

3/4 cup (90 g) crumbled blue or Gorgonzola cheese

Preheat oven to 350°F (180°C, or gas mark 4). Evenly coat a 9" × 13" (22.5 x 32.5 cm) baking dish with cooking spray or olive oil. In a large pot of boiling, salted water, cook the lasagna noodles until al dente, about 10 minutes. Drain and rinse under cold water, and set aside on a towel to dry.

[For chicken mixture]
In a large skillet over medium to high heat, melt the butter and oil. Sauté the onion, garlic, and peppers until tender and onions become translucent, about 5 minutes. Add chicken and cayenne pepper, stir, and cook for an additional 2 minutes. Add vinegar, Worcestershire sauce,

and Thai curry paste, stir, and continue to cook for another minute. Add tomato sauce and water, bring to a boil for 1 minute, add hot sauce, reduce heat, and allow to cook for 10 more minutes. Remove from heat and set aside. In a medium mixing bowl, combine the beaten egg with the ricotta cheese and set aside.

[To assemble]
Layer the bottom of the baking dish with three lasagna noodles, top with 1¹/₂ cups (300 g) of the chicken mixture and half of the ricotta cheese mixture, and sprinkle with half of the mozzarella cheese. Top with three more noodles and repeat with 1¹/₂ cups (300 g) chicken mixture, remaining ricotta cheese, and remaining mozzarella cheese. Top with one last layer of lasagna noodles and remaining chicken mixture. Cover pan and bake for 30 minutes. Remove cover, sprinkle crumbled blue cheese on top, and bake an additional 10 minutes until top is golden and bubbly. Remove from oven and let rest for 10 minutes before cutting to serve.

Asparagus and Mascarpone
Chicken Roulades

Roulades are a great, elegant, make-ahead meal, easy
to warm and serve at a later time. The creaminess of the
cheese filling is a great complement to the sautéed fennel
sauce and melted Gruyère cheese.

6 (6-ounce [170-g]) boneless, skinless chicken breasts, pounded to 1/4" (6.25 mm) thickness

Salt and pepper

1/4 cup (60 g) mascarpone cheese

1/3 cup (85 g) ricotta cheese

1 cup (110 g) shredded Gruyère cheese, divided

2 tablespoons (5 g) chopped fresh basil

SAUCE

2 thick slices pancetta, chopped

4 tablespoons (56 g) butter

1 head fennel, cleaned, cut in half, sliced thin

1/2 pound (225 g) asparagus, thinly sliced on the diagonal

Juice of 2 lemons

1/4 cup (60 ml) chicken stock or broth

1 teaspoon (8 mg) fresh chopped thyme

1 can (14.5 ounces [411 g]) diced tomatoes

6 thin slices (about 1/4 pound [115 g]) prosciutto

1 pound (455 g) asparagus spears, cut into 4" (10-cm) lengths

2 tablespoons (30 ml) olive oil

To pound the chicken, lay plastic wrap out on a flat surface. Slice chicken breasts in half lengthwise, folding outward like wings as you go, being careful not to slice all the way through. Place breasts on plastic wrap, folding plastic wrap over the chicken. Pound the breast using a kitchen mallet, evenly, until 1/4" (6.25 mm) thick. Repeat with each chicken breast. Season each breast with salt and pepper and set aside. In a small mixing bowl, combine the mascarpone and ricotta cheeses with 1/2 cup (55 g) shredded Gruyère cheese and chopped basil. Season with salt and pepper and stir to combine thoroughly. To prepare the sauce, render the fat from the pancetta by frying over medium-high heat. Remove cooked pancetta, add butter to skillet, and melt. Add fennel and diagonally sliced asparagus, sauté until soft, about 5 minutes. Add lemon juice and chicken stock, deglazing the pan. Add thyme and tomatoes, sauté for 5 minutes, remove from heat, and set aside. Begin making roulades by laying chicken out flat. Place 1 slice prosciutto in the middle of each breast, topping with about 2 tablespoons (30 g) cheese filling and 4 asparagus spears. To form roulades, fold in sides of the breast and roll away from you. Set each roulade aside until all are complete. In a large skillet, melt 2 tablespoons (28 g) butter with 2 tablespoons (28 ml) olive oil over medium heat. Add chicken roulades to hot skillet, browning on all sides. Remove, transferring to a 9" × 13" (22.5 × 32.5 cm) baking dish. If your skillet isn't large enough, brown the roulades in batches, adding more butter and oil as needed. Once all roulades are browned and in the baking dish, top with fennel sauce. If preparing roulades to serve at a later time, prepare to this point, wrap in plastic wrap, and refrigerate until ready to use, up to 5 days. Or, wrap tightly with plastic wrap and then with heavy-duty aluminum foil and freeze for up to 1 month. To serve, remove from refrigerator and bring to room temperature for about 20 minutes. If the roulades appear to be a bit dry, add 1/2 cup (120 ml) chicken stock. Preheat oven to 375°F (190°C, or gas mark 5). Bake for 30 minutes. Remove from oven, change oven to broiler mode. Top chicken roulades with remaining 1/2 cup shredded Gruyère cheese, place under broiler, and melt until golden, about 3 minutes. Remove and serve. If baking from frozen state, transfer roulades to refrigerator and thaw overnight, then follow above directions for baking.

chapter 4

Ethnic One-Dish Flavors

[serves 4 to 6]

Lobster **Cannelloni with** Crab **and Cognac Cream**

Stuffed pasta is great for freezing for later preparation. When ready to use, place in the refrigerator, thaw, and place in a baking dish; then top with the sauce and bake.

1 package (8 ounces [225 g]) cannelloni or manicotti shells

3 tablespoons (45 g) butter

3 cloves garlic, minced

3 shallots, minced

3 cups (about 1 1/2 pounds [680 g]) finely chopped cooked lobster meat

1 cup (200 g) cooked crabmeat

1/4 cup (60 ml) cognac

1 container (8 ounces [225 g]) whipped cream cheese

1 container (8 ounces [225 g]) ricotta cheese

1/4 cup (25 g) freshly grated Parmesan cheese

1/2 cup (60 g) shredded mozzarella cheese

3 tablespoons (9 g) chopped chives

3 tablespoons (12 g) chopped fresh tarragon

Salt and black pepper

Chopped fresh parsley and tarragon for garnish

CRAB AND COGNAC CREAM

4 tablespoons (55 g) unsalted butter

3 shallots, chopped

10 ounces (280 g) oyster mushrooms, chopped

8 ounces (225 g) whole chunk Maryland crabmeat

1/2 cup (120 ml) cognac

1/2 cup (75 g) diced seeded tomato

2 1/2 cups (570 ml) heavy cream

1/4 cup (25 g) grated Parmesan cheese

Salt and black pepper

Cook the cannelloni in a large pot of boiling salted water until al dente, about 12 minutes; drain and set aside. In a large skillet over medium-high heat, melt the butter; add the garlic and shallots, sautéing until tender, about 4 minutes. Add lobster and crabmeat, cooking for 3 minutes. Add cognac and cook for 4 minutes, reducing by half. Remove from heat and set aside to cool. Once cool, stir together with the cream cheese, ricotta cheese, Parmesan cheese, mozzarella cheese, chives, and tarragon; season with salt and black pepper. Cut the pasta shells open lengthwise. Spoon about 1/2 cup (120 g) lobster/crab stuffing into each shell and press the cut sides together. Place stuffed cannelloni cut-side down in a 9" × 13" (22.5 × 32.5 cm) baking dish. Spoon Crab and Cognac Cream (recipe follows) evenly over shells. Bake, covered, at 350°F (180°C, or gas mark 4) for 25 to 30 minutes, until thoroughly heated through. Garnish with chopped parsley and tarragon.

[For Crab and Cognac Cream]
Melt the butter in a skillet over medium-high heat. Add the shallots and mushrooms and sauté until the mushrooms are wilted and the shallots are tender, about 7 minutes. Add the crabmeat and cook for 3 minutes. Add the cognac and reduce by half; add the tomato, heavy cream, and Parmesan cheese. Cook until thickened, about 7 minutes; season with salt and black pepper.

[serves 6]

Thai Lasagna with Stir-Fried Vegetables and Curried Tofu

All the flavors of pad thai are combined with crisp, fresh Asian vegetables and a creamy tofu filling to create a truly Eastern approach to lasagna.

8 fresh or dried lasagna noodles

3 tablespoons (45 ml) Thai fish sauce

3 tablespoons (45 ml) fresh lime juice

2 tablespoons (28 g) sugar

1 tablespoon (14 ml) sesame oil

1 tablespoon (14 ml) olive oil

4 green onions, sliced diagonally

1/2 cup (60 g) shredded carrot

2 cloves garlic, minced

1 1/2 cups (75 g) bean sprouts

1 (1 1/2 pound [670 g]) head bok choy, cleaned and trimmed, cut in half lengthwise and then chopped

1/4 teaspoon (.5 g) red pepper flakes

1 tablespoon (4 g) fresh cilantro, chopped, plus additional left whole for garnish

2 tablespoons (28 g) chopped dry roasted peanuts

2 pounds (1 kg) soft tofu, drained

2 tablespoons (8 g) fresh flat-leaf parsley, minced

2 tablespoons (5 g) fresh basil, minced

1/2 teaspoon (1.25 g) turmeric

2 tablespoons (30 g) Thai curry paste

1/4 cup (60 ml) coconut milk, not shaken

2 tablespoons (28 g) sugar

Preheat oven to 400°F (200°C, or gas mark 6). Oil the inside of a 9" × 13" (22.5 × 32.5 cm) baking dish. In a large pot of boiling, salted water cook the lasagna noodles, 10 minutes for dry and 2 to 3 minutes for fresh. Remove the noodles from the water and rinse in cold water. Place the noodles on a paper towel to dry. In a small mixing bowl, combine the fish sauce, lime juice, and sugar; set the mixture aside. Heat the sesame and olive oils in a large skillet over medium to high heat. Add the onion, carrots, and garlic, and stir-fry the vegetables until tender, about 2 minutes, being careful not to brown them. Add the bean sprouts and bok choy, combine, and cook for an additional 2 to 4 minutes until wilted. Add the pepper flakes, cilantro, and peanuts, and cook for 1 additional minute. Add the fish sauce mixture, combine, and cook until the liquid is reduced by half, about 5 minutes.

Place the tofu in the bowl of a food processor fitted with the blade attachment. Process the tofu until uniform and creamy. Add the parsley, basil, turmeric, curry paste, coconut milk, and sugar. Process until well combined. Remove the mixture from the processor and set aside.

[To assemble]
Place two sheets of pasta on the bottom of your baking dish, cutting them to fit if necessary. Top with the vegetable mixture, then another layer of pasta, then the tofu mixture. Repeat the layers with pasta, vegetable mixture, pasta, and finally the tofu mixture on top. Place in the oven and bake for 20 minutes, or until it begins to turn golden brown and crack. Remove from the oven and let rest for 10 minutes before cutting to serve.

Smoked Chicken Enchiladas with Green Chile Sauce

This dish can be made with grilled, poached, sautéed, or baked chicken. However, smoking the chicken adds a flavor unparalleled by the others. Making this dish ahead of time provides a great meal for a day or night when time just isn't on your side.

2 tablespoons (28 g) butter	2 teaspoons (3 g) dried oregano
2 large onions, thinly sliced	1 teaspoon (2.5 g) ground cumin
1 teaspoon (5 g) sugar	1/2 teaspoon (1.25 g) paprika
2 cups (280 g) chopped smoked chicken	11/4 cups (295 ml) chicken stock
1/4 teaspoon (1.5 g) salt	2 packages (3 ounces [85 g] each) cream cheese, cubed
1/4 teaspoon (5 mg) pepper	1/2 cup (120 g) sour cream
4 cans (4.5 ounces [130 g] each) diced green chiles	1/2 cup (120 g) diced canned tomatoes
1 chipotle chile in adobo sauce, diced	2 cups (8 ounces [225 g]) shredded Cheddar cheese
1 small onion, chopped	1 cup (4 ounces [115 g]) shredded Monterey Jack cheese
3 green onions, green tops only, chopped	10 (7" [17.5-cm]) flour tortillas
2 garlic cloves, minced	3 tablespoons (12 g) chopped fresh cilantro garnish

Preheat oven to 375°F (190°C, or gas mark 5). Melt the butter in a large skillet over medium-high heat, stirring often; add the sliced onions, cook for 5 minutes until just becoming tender. Reduce heat to low, sprinkle with sugar, stir and cook for an additional 20 minutes, caramelizing the onions until golden brown. Add the chopped smoked chicken and salt and pepper; stir to combine and set aside. In the bowl of a food processor fitted with the blade attachment, combine the green chiles with the chipotle chile, onion, green onions, garlic, oregano, cumin, and paprika; pulse until well combined and chopped. Bring chile mixture and chicken stock to a boil in a saucepan over high heat; cook 5 minutes, until thickened. Add cream cheese and cook until cheese is melted. Remove from heat, add sour cream and diced tomato. In a small bowl, combine the shredded Cheddar cheese with the shredded Monterey Jack cheese, tossing to combine.

Spread one-third chile mixture evenly on bottom of a lightly greased 9" × 13" (22.5 × 32.5 cm) baking dish. Working on a clean, flat surface, lay out flour tortillas. Spoon chicken mixture evenly down the center of each tortilla; top with a pinch of shredded cheese (reserving half of the cheese for the top), roll, and place seam-side down in the baking dish. Repeat with all tortillas, placing them side by side in baking dish, fitting them tightly. Top with remaining chile mixture; sprinkle with remaining cheeses. Place on middle rack of oven and bake at 375°F (190°C, or gas mark 5) for 20 to 25 minutes, until bubbling and cheese is melted and begins to brown. Remove, sprinkle with chopped cilantro, and serve.

This dish may be made ahead of time, then covered tightly with plastic wrap and refrigerated until ready to bake, for up to 4 days.

To freeze, prepare dish as directed, cover tightly with plastic wrap and then with aluminum foil, and freeze for up to 1 month. To bake, transfer from freezer to refrigerator and thaw for 24 hours, then bake as directed above.

[serves 8]

Mexican Black Bean Lasagna

Replacing lasagna noodles with tender corn tortillas gives a Southwestern twist to an Italian classic. The use of black beans keeps down the calories, while fresh vegetables and spices impart great flavors. Olé!

1 pound (455 g) chicken breasts, cooked and cut into chunks

2 tablespoons (28 ml) olive oil

1/2 cup (65 g) chopped onion

1/2 cup (65 g) chopped red bell pepper

1/2 cup (65 g) frozen corn kernels, thawed

2 cloves garlic, chopped

1 1/2 teaspoons (3.75 g) ground cumin

1 teaspoon (2.5 g) chili powder

1 (15-ounce [440 ml]) can black beans, rinsed and drained

1 (16-ounce [455 g]) can refried black beans

2 cups (475 ml) canned tomato sauce

1/2 cup (113 g) salsa

1 (10-ounce [285 ml]) can enchilada sauce

1/4 cup (15 g) chopped fresh cilantro

9 corn tortillas

8 ounces (225 g) shredded cheddar cheese

6 ounces (170 g) shredded Monterey Jack cheese

1/4 cup (25 g) sliced black olives (optional)

1/4 cup (83 g) sour cream for garnish

8 sprigs fresh cilantro for garnish

Preheat oven to 350°F (180°C, or gas mark 4). Spray the sides and bottom of a 9" × 13" (22.5 × 32.5 cm) baking dish with nonstick cooking spray. In a medium saucepan, bring an ample amount of water to a boil to cook the chicken. Boil the chicken for about 10 minutes until cooked through.

Remove from water and set aside to cool. Once it is cool to the touch, chop the chicken into small chunks. In a large skillet on medium-high heat, heat the olive oil. Add the onion, pepper, corn, and garlic. Sauté the vegetables until they are wilted and translucent, about 10 minutes. Add the cumin and chili powder. Continue to cook for an additional 2 minutes. Add the black beans and chicken. Stir to incorporate flavors and heat through.

Remove the mixture from the heat and set aside. Place a medium-sized saucepan on medium heat and add the refried beans, tomato sauce, salsa, enchilada sauce, and fresh cilantro. Heat to a boil and remove from the heat.

[To assemble]
Place one-third of the tomato sauce mixture on the bottom of the baking dish; cover with three tortillas. Top the tortillas with half of the chicken mixture then another one-third of the sauce, topping this with half of the Cheddar cheese. Repeat the layers with three tortillas, the remaining chicken mixture, sauce, and Cheddar cheese, then top all this with three more tortillas, Monterey Jack cheese, and sliced black olives. Place in the oven uncovered, and bake for 20 to 30 minutes until the top is browned and bubbly. Remove from oven and let rest for 10 minutes before cutting to serve. To serve, place the lasagna on a plate, put a tablespoon of sour cream on top, and garnish with a sprig of cilantro.

Baked Chicken **and** Gnocchi Marsala

I love the rich and creamy flavor of Marsala wine with tender chicken breast. The delicious, firm bite of the gnocchi pairs well with the elegant flavors of the Marsala sauce.

2 packages (16 ounces [455 g] each) frozen gnocchi

1 cup (125 g) all-purpose flour, divided

1/2 teaspoon (3 g) salt

1/2 teaspoon (1 g) freshly ground black pepper

1 1/2 pounds (680 g) boneless, skinless chicken breast, cut into thin strips

1/4 cup (60 ml) extra-virgin olive oil, more if needed

1/4 cup (55 g) butter

1 jar (15 ounces [420 g]) whole white pearl onions, drained

1 package (10 ounces [280 g]) cremini or baby bella mushrooms, stems removed, chopped

2 cups (475 ml) Marsala wine

1 1/2 cups (355 ml) chicken stock

1 teaspoon (8 mg) chopped fresh thyme

2 1/2 cups (275 g) shredded Gruyère cheese, divided

Cook gnocchi in a large pot of salted boiling water for 5 minutes, drain, and set aside in a large bowl. In a medium-sized shallow dish, combine 3/4 cup (95 g) flour with 1/2 teaspoon (3 g) salt and 1/2 teaspoon (1 g) black pepper, stirring with a fork to combine. Toss sliced chicken in the flour, coating evenly; shake pieces to dust off any excess flour and set aside. In a large skillet, heat the olive oil over medium-high heat; add the chicken and sauté until browned on all sides, 7 to 8 minutes. Remove, transferring to a paper towel–lined plate to drain. Add butter to the skillet. Once melted, add onions and mushrooms and cook for 3 minutes; add remaining 1/4 cup (30 g) flour, cooking for 3 additional minutes, stirring to prevent burning. Add the Marsala, chicken stock, and thyme to the skillet, stirring and cooking for 3 additional minutes, until thick. Remove from heat and pour over the cooked gnocchi.

Preheat oven to 375°F (190°C, or gas mark 5). Add the chicken and 1 cup (110 g) of the shredded cheese to the gnocchi mixture. Pour into a greased 9" × 13" (22.5 × 32.5-cm) casserole, top with remaining shredded cheese, and bake for 20 minutes. Remove and serve.

Spice-Braised Salmon with Mixed Bean Ragout

Salmon is an excellent, versatile fish that people don't seem to enjoy often enough. I have to confess, it wasn't until recently that I have really begun to experiment with salmon. I share this recipe with you after having enjoyed a similar dish in the Caribbean.

DRY RUB

$1/2$ teaspoon (1 g) caraway seeds

$1/2$ teaspoon (1 g) fennel seeds

$1/2$ teaspoon (1 g) cumin seeds

1 teaspoon (1.6 g) green peppercorns

1 teaspoon (6 g) sea salt

1 teaspoon (2 g) coarsely ground black pepper

$1/2$ teaspoon (1 g) curry powder

1 (3-pound [1.4-kg]) boneless salmon fillet, skinned and cut into 6 steaks

6 tablespoons (90 ml) olive oil, divided

1 small Vidalia onion, diced

1 red pepper, diced

1 green pepper, diced

1 rib celery, diced

$1/4$ cup (60 ml) dry white wine

3 cloves garlic, minced

4 cups (940 ml) vegetable stock

3 bay leaves

$1^{1}/_{2}$ tablespoons (3.75 g) chopped fresh lemon thyme

1 can (15.5 ounces [439 g]) butter beans, drained

1 can (15.5 ounces [439 g]) navy beans, drained

1 can (15.5 ounces [439 g]) pink beans, drained

1 can (15.5 ounces [439 g]) green pigeon peas, drained

2 lemons (1 cut into 6 thin slices; 1 cut into 6 wedges for garnish)

In a small mortar and pestle or a spice grinder, combine the caraway seeds, fennel seeds, cumin seeds, green peppercorns, sea salt, and coarsely ground black pepper. Grind to a coarse consistency. Add the curry powder and combine. Rub each side of the salmon steaks generously and evenly with the dry rub. Set aside for 30 minutes or cover and refrigerate for up to 2 hours. If refrigerating, remove 30 minutes prior to cooking.

Preheat oven to 400°F (200°C, or gas mark 6). Heat 4 tablespoons (60 ml) olive oil in a 13" (32.5-cm) ovenproof skillet over medium-high heat. Once smoking, add salmon fillets in an even layer, skinned-side down, searing on each side, about 3 minutes per side, until well browned. Transfer to a plate and set aside. Add remaining 2 tablespoons (28 ml) olive oil to the pan. Once hot, add the

onion, peppers, and celery; sauté for 5 minutes, until tender. Add wine and garlic; deglaze the pan by scraping up any bits from the sides and bottom of the skillet. Reduce wine until almost gone. Add vegetable stock, bay leaves, lemon thyme, beans, and pigeon peas, cooking and stirring for 3 minutes. Return salmon fillets to the skillet, top with lemon slices, and transfer to the middle rack of the oven. Bake, uncovered, for 45 minutes, until salmon is golden-pink on top and flaky. Serve with wild rice atop bean ragout with a lemon wedge garnish.

Stir-Fried Shrimp with Blood Orange and Ponzu Sauce

A favorite cooking vessel of mine is the wok, and using it for one-dish cooking is an obvious choice. If you are planning a meal ahead, clean, cut, and chop your ingredients the day before, then stir-fry a superb, quick dinner.

2 pounds (905 g) large shrimp (16/20 size), peeled and deveined

1/2 cup (120 ml) ponzu sauce (available in the Asian section of your supermarket)

2 teaspoons (3 g) orange zest

3/4 cup (175 ml) freshly squeezed orange juice

1/4 cup (60 ml) pineapple juice, plus 2 tablespoons (28 ml)

1 tablespoon (6 g) coarsely ground black pepper

1 pound (455 g) monkfish, skinned, cut into large chunks

4 tablespoons (60 ml) peanut oil, divided

1/2 pound (225 g) snow peas, strings removed, sliced thin

1/2 pound (225 g) broccolini, ends trimmed, chopped rough

2 cups (140 g) chopped shiitake mushrooms

3 cloves garlic, minced

6 blood oranges, segmented, juices reserved

1 bunch chives chopped into 2" (5-cm) lengths

1 tablespoon (8 g) cornstarch dissolved in 1 tablespoon (15 ml) cold water

2 tablespoons (28 ml) Asian chile-garlic sauce

Wash the shrimp and pat dry. In a large nonreactive mixing bowl, combine 1/4 cup (60 ml) ponzu sauce, orange zest, 1/2 cup (120 ml) orange juice, 1/4 cup (60 ml) pineapple juice, and black pepper; stir to combine. Add shrimp and monkfish to the marinade, cover, and refrigerate for at least 30 minutes and up to 2 hours. Heat 2 tablespoons (28 ml) peanut oil in a wok over high heat. Once hot, add the shrimp and monkfish, drained from the marinade, and stir-fry until the fish is opaque white and the shrimp are just turning pink and curled, about 6 minutes; remove and set aside. Add remaining 2 tablespoons (28 ml) peanut oil to the wok. Once hot, add the snow peas, broccolini, mushrooms, and garlic; stir-fry for 4 minutes, add the blood oranges and chives, toss to heat through. Return shrimp and monkfish with remaining orange and pineapple juices to the wok, bring to a boil, and add the cornstarch-water mixture; stir to thicken. Add Asian chile-garlic sauce and season with salt and pepper. Serve hot with rice or glass noodles.

[serves 4]

Braised Tropical Chicken with Pineapple, Mango, and Cloves

When braising, food is browned in fat then cooked in a small amount of liquid for a long period of time. Tough cuts of meat, such as beef, pork roasts, or lamb shanks are made more tender by braising. I have paired the tropical flavors of pineapple and mango and the punch of cloves with whole chicken pieces, cooked until the meat just falls from the bone.

1/3 cup (40 g) all-purpose flour

1/2 teaspoon (1 g) salt

1/2 teaspoon (.5 g) freshly ground pepper

1/2 teaspoon (1 g) ground cloves

1/2 teaspoon (1 g) ground cardamom

1 chicken (3–4 pounds [1.4–1.9 kg]), cut into 8 serving pieces

3 tablespoons (45 ml) extra-virgin olive oil

1 yellow onion, thinly sliced

8 ounces (225 g) white button mushrooms, quartered

4 scallions, white and green parts chopped into 2" (5-cm) pieces

1 cup (235 ml) sweet white wine, such as Riesling

2 tablespoons (28 ml) dark rum

1/2 cup (120 ml) chicken stock

1/2 cup (120 ml) mango nectar

3 cloves garlic, crushed

1/2 cup (90 g) chopped mango

1/2 cup (75 g) chopped fresh golden pineapple

Zest and juice of 1 lime

1/4 cup (15 g) chopped fresh cilantro

2 sprigs fresh mint

1/2 teaspoon (1 g) ground turmeric

2 bay leaves

Salt and freshly ground black pepper

Preheat an oven to 375°F (190°C, or gas mark 5).

In a large bowl, combine the flour, salt, pepper, cloves, and cardamom. Add the chicken and toss to coat evenly.

In a deep-sided sauté pan or cast-iron Dutch oven over medium heat, warm the olive oil. Add half of the chicken and brown on all sides, 3 to 4 minutes total. Transfer to a plate. Brown the remaining chicken and transfer to the plate.

Add the onion, mushrooms, and scallions to the pan and cook, stirring occasionally, until golden, about 5 minutes. Add the wine, dark rum, chicken stock, and mango nectar. Increase the heat to high and bring to a boil, stirring for about 5 minutes.

Return the chicken to the pan and add the garlic, mango, pineapple, lime juice and zest, cilantro, mint, turmeric, and bay leaves. Bring to a boil, cover, and transfer to the oven. Cook until the chicken is very tender, about 45 minutes. Season with salt and pepper, remove the mint sprigs and bay leaf, and serve immediately.

JERK MARINADE

1/4 cup (15 g) cilantro leaves

1/2 cup (30 g) flat-leaf
parsley leaves

1/2 bunch scallions, chopped

8 mint leaves

1/4 cup (35 g) garlic cloves,
rough chopped

1/4 cup (25 g) chopped ginger

1/4 cup (20 g) dried orange peel

1 tablespoon (7 g) ground
cinnamon

1/2 tablespoon (3.5 g)
five-spice powder

1 teaspoon (2 g) ground allspice

2 habanero chiles

1/2 cup (120 ml) hoisin sauce

Juice of 2 limes

2 cups (475 ml) canola oil

1 (4-pound [1.9-kg])
boned pork loin, trimmed and
cleaned, patted dry

1/4 cup (60 ml) vegetable oil

1 large yellow onion, chopped

1 red bell pepper, seeded and
chopped

1 yellow bell pepper, seeded
and chopped

2 cups (300 g) chopped
yellow turnip

3 cloves garlic, crushed

2 cups (140 g) shaved red cabbage

2 cups (140 g) shaved
white cabbage

1 cup (160 g) seedless
red grapes, halved

1 cup (235 ml) dry red wine

1/2 cup (120 ml) chicken
stock or water

1/2 cup (120 ml) cider vinegar

1/4 cup (60 g) packed brown sugar

ORANGE SYRUP

1 cup (300 g) orange marmalade

1/4 cup (60 g) dark rum

1/2 cup (120 ml) water

1 tablespoon (8 g) freshly
grated ginger

1 teaspoon (2 g) orange zest

[serves 6]

Jerked Pork Loin **with Braised Sweet and Sour Cabbage**

Jerk is a technique developed in Jamaica to marinate or season meat, usually pork and chicken. Jerk seasoning is a combination of flavorful, aromatic herbs and spices that impart a unique, vibrant flavor to meats. Enjoy this dish with the braised cabbage and red grapes alongside a bed of white rice or polenta.

Puree cilantro, parsley, scallions, mint, garlic, ginger, and orange peel in a food processor. Add a little of the canola oil if necessary. Add the spices and chiles and puree. Add the hoisin and lime juice; while the machine is running, add the canola oil in a steady stream. Remove marinade from processor, reserving ¼ cup (60 ml). Place pork loin in a deep nonreactive bowl and pour marinade over, cover, and marinate, refrigerated, overnight.

Heat the vegetable oil in a large, deep skillet or cast-iron Dutch oven over medium-high heat. Remove the pork from the marinade and place in skillet, browning on all sides. Transfer pork to a plate. Add the onion, red pepper, and yellow pepper to the hot pan and cook until tender, about 5 minutes. Add the turnip and garlic and cook for 8 minutes. Add the red and white cabbage, red grapes, wine, stock, vinegar, and brown sugar; stir to combine. Bring to a boil and cook for 8 minutes. Add the pork back to the pan, cover, and place in hot oven. Bake for 1 to 1½ hours, until the pork is tender and the cabbage is cooked down, basting with reserved marinade every 15 minutes. Remove, let rest for 5 minutes, slice, and serve drizzled with Orange Syrup.

[For Orange Syrup]
In a nonreactive saucepan over medium heat, combine all the ingredients and bring to a boil; reduce the heat and cook for 5 minutes, until thick. Remove and store in an airtight container until ready to use. Warm and serve.

[serves 6]

Spider Beef with Sticky Jasmine Rice

I call this Spider Beef simply because the sliced beef reminds me of long spider legs. Also, I always feel that Asian dishes have the most colorful names—this is my contribution.

4 cups (950 ml) water

1 teaspoon (6 g) kosher salt

1½ cups (290 g) jasmine rice

2 pounds (905 g) beef top round, sliced into thin strips

1 tablespoon (6 g) coarsely cracked black pepper

3 ¼ teaspoon (1.5 g) Chinese five-spice powder

½ teaspoon (2.5 ml) sesame oil

1 tablespoon (15 ml) soy sauce, plus an additional ¼ cup (60 ml)

4 cloves garlic, minced

2 tablespoons (28 ml) hoisin sauce

2 tablespoons (28 ml) black bean sauce

1 tablespoon (8 g) cornstarch

1 tablespoon (15 ml) water

¼ cup (60 ml) beef broth

¼ cup (60 ml) vegetable oil

1 red bell pepper, seeded and chopped

1 yellow bell pepper, seeded and chopped

1 orange bell pepper, seeded and chopped

5 green onions, coarsely chopped

1 Granny Smith apple, peeled, cored, and coarsely chopped, tossed in 1 teaspoon (5 ml) lime juice

2 tablespoons (5 g) fresh basil, cut chiffonade-style

In a large saucepot, bring the water to a boil with the salt. Add the rice, stir, and cover; reduce heat to a simmer and cook until stiff and sticky—about 30 to 40 minutes. Set aside, keeping warm.

Place the beef in a bowl, sprinkle with black pepper and Chinese five-spice powder. Add sesame oil, 1 tablespoon (15 ml) soy sauce, and garlic; toss to coat evenly, cover, and let marinate for at least 30 minutes and up to 4 hours, refrigerated.

In a small bowl, combine the remaining soy sauce, hoisin sauce, and black bean sauce; set aside. In a separate bowl, combine the cornstarch with the water, stirring with a fork to dissolve. Add to beef broth, stir, and set aside.

Heat the vegetable oil in a wok over high heat. Once very hot, add the red, yellow, and orange peppers; green onions; and apple; stir-fry for 2 minutes. Add the beef with the marinade and stir-fry until cooked through, about 5 minutes. Add basil and black bean sauce mixture, bring to a boil, add cornstarch-and-broth mixture; stir to thicken sauce.

Form rice into individual molds on plates and top with Spider Beef stir-fry.

[serves 9]

Bourbon Street Lasagna with Cornbread Crust

Straight from New Orleans, this intensely flavored dish, topped with a unique cornbread crust, is easy to make and delicious. I have combined cayenne pepper, chili paste, and hot pepper sauce with garden-fresh vegetables to create this truly Creole experience. The cornbread topping browns to a dense, moist crust.

9 sheets fresh or dried lasagna noodles

6 tablespoons (90 ml) vegetable or olive oil

2 stalks celery, chopped

1 green bell pepper, chopped

1 red bell pepper, chopped

1/2 onion, chopped

1 cup (130 g) frozen corn kernels, thawed

2 cups (120 g) fresh okra, sliced

1 1/2 tablespoons (3.75 g) fresh thyme leaves, chopped, or 2 1/2 teaspoons (3 g) dried

1 1/2 tablespoons (3.75 g) fresh sage leaves, chopped, or 2 1/2 teaspoons (3 g) dried

1 1/2 tablespoons (2.5 g) fresh rosemary, chopped, or 2 1/2 teaspoons (2 g) dried

1 to 2 cups (235–475 ml) water

1 cup (225 g) chopped boneless, skinless chicken breasts

7 ounces (190 g) smoked sausage (such as andouille), sliced into fourths, then into chunks

CREOLE SAUCE

6 tablespoons (80 g) unsalted butter

1/2 cup (55 g) all-purpose flour

2 cups (475 ml) chicken or vegetable stock or canned broth

2 cups (475 ml) Quick Tomato Sauce (see page 65)

1 teaspoon (3 g) chile powder

1/2 teaspoon (1.25 g) cayenne pepper

1 teaspoon chili (5 g) paste or Thai curry paste

1 teaspoon (2 g) coarsly ground black pepper

1/2 teaspoon (3 ml) hot sauce

CORNBREAD TOPPING

1/2 cup (138 g) coarse yellow cornmeal

1 1/2 cups (170 g) all-purpose flour

1/3 cup (75 g) firmly packed light brown sugar

1 teaspoon (1.5 g) baking powder

1/4 teaspoon (.4 g) baking soda

1/2 teaspoon (3 g) salt

1/2 teaspoon (1.25 g) ground coriander

1 large egg, lightly beaten

1 1/2 cups (355 ml) buttermilk

1/4 cup (60 ml) vegetable oil

FOR ASSEMBLY

4 ounces (115 g) shredded mozzarella cheese

4 ounces (115 g) shredded Monterey Jack cheese

Preheat oven to 375°F (190°C, or gas mark 5. Oil the sides and bottom of a 9" × 13" (22.5 x 32.5 cm) baking dish. In a large stockpot of boiling, salted water, cook the noodles until al dente, about 10 minutes for dry, 2 to 3 minutes for fresh. Drain the pasta, rinse with cold water, and set aside on paper towels to dry. In a large skillet on medium-high heat, add 4 tablespoons (60 ml) of olive oil. When the oil is hot, add the celery, green pepper, red pepper, and onion. Sauté until translucent and tender, about 5 minutes. Add the corn and continue to cook for an additional 2 minutes, then add the okra. Stir the okra into the mixture and continue to cook. The okra will begin to get gummy and possibly stick to the bottom of the pan. If the skillet appears to be dry and the vegetables are sticking, add 1 cup (235 ml) of water to moisten.

Continue to cook until the okra is tender and bright green in color, about 5 minutes. Add the thyme, sage, and rosemary. At this point, if the mixture appears to be overly dry, again add up to 1 cup (235 ml) of water and cook until a thick liquid forms. Remove the skillet from the heat and set it aside. In a separate medium skillet, heat the remaining 2 tablespoons (28 ml) of oil on medium to high heat. Add the chicken and sausage, and cook until browned and cooked through, about 10 minutes. Add the chicken and sausage to the vegetable mixture and combine.

[To prepare the Creole sauce]
In a medium saucepan over medium to high heat, melt the butter and add the flour; using a whisk, stir continuously, cooking the roux until a rich, dark brown color with a nutty aroma, about 5–7 minutes. This is the roux (thickener) for the sauce. Add the chicken stock 1/2 cup (120 ml) at a time, stirring vigorously after each addition to prevent lumps. Be careful of the initial steam that will rise from adding the chicken stock. After all the chicken stock is incorporated, reduce the heat to low and add the tomato sauce; stir and cook for 5 minutes. Add the chili powder, cayenne pepper, chili paste, black pepper, and hot sauce, stir to incorporate, and continue to cook for 5 minutes. Remove the saucepan from the heat and set it aside.

[To prepare cornbread topping]
In a medium-sized mixing bowl, combine all the dry ingredients; using a whisk, stir them until thoroughly mixed. Pushing from the middle of the bowl outward with a spoon, form a well in the center of the dry ingredients. Add the egg, buttermilk, and oil in the well. Working from the sides inward with the whisk, begin to incorporate the dry ingredients gradually, then whisk vigorously to combine the ingredients. The slow incorporation of the wet ingredients into the dry will prevent lumps from forming in the batter. Set aside for assembly.

[To assemble]
In your baking dish, place 1 1/2 cups (355 ml) of Creole sauce, evenly coating the bottom of the pan; top with three sheets of noodles. Top noodles with half of the vegetable filling, and sprinkle with half of the mozzarella and Monterey Jack cheeses. Repeat the layers with pasta, then 1 1/2 cups (355 ml) of sauce, pasta again, the remainder of the vegetable filling, and finally the remainder of the cheese. Using your hands, firmly pack the lasagna layers in the pan, making room for the cornbread batter on top. Drizzle the cornbread batter over the top in a solid layer, evenly coating the top layer. You may not need all of the batter; this depends on the thickness of your layers. Place the baking dish on a large cookie sheet to catch any drippings. Bake on middle rack of the oven, uncovered, for 20 minutes, or until the cornbread topping is golden brown and firm to the touch. The sides will be bubbling. Remove from the oven and let rest for 10 minutes before serving. There should be remaining Creole sauce that can be heated and served over the top of each portion of lasagna.

Shrimp and Mango Pad Thai with Cashews

Tender, juicy shrimp are combined with mouthwatering, sweet mangoes to make a great pad thai that will be enjoyed by all.

2 tablespoons (28 ml) vegetable oil

4 cloves garlic, minced

1 teaspoon (2.5 g) freshly grated ginger

2 pounds (905 g) jumbo shrimp, peeled and deveined

1 red bell pepper, seeded, sliced thin

1 yellow bell pepper, seeded, sliced thin

4 scallions, sliced thin diagonally

6 ounces (170 g) shiitake mushrooms, stems removed, sliced thin

1 ripe mango, peeled and sliced thin

1/2 teaspoon (1 g) minced fresh mint

1 tablespoon (4 g) chopped fresh cilantro, plus extra for garnish

1/4 pound (115 g) medium-wide rice noodles, soaked in warm water until softened, drained

2 tablespoons (28 ml) Asian fish sauce

1/4 cup (60 ml) lime juice

1 tablespoon (15 ml) cider vinegar

2 tablespoons (30 g) packed brown sugar

1 teaspoon (5 g) Asian chile paste

Salt and pepper

1/2 cup (65 g) chopped roasted cashews

Lime wedges for garnish

Place a large aluminum or cast-iron wok over medium-high heat, add 2 tablespoons (28 ml) vegetable oil. When hot, add the garlic and ginger, cook for 1 minute, until fragrant. Add the shrimp, red pepper, yellow pepper, scallions, and shiitake mushrooms; cook for 3 minutes, until the vegetables are tender and the shrimp is pink. Add the mango, mint, and cilantro, and cook for 2 minutes. Add the noodles, fish sauce, lime juice, cider vinegar, brown sugar, and chile paste; toss vigorously to combine, and allow sauce to thicken for 1 minute. Season with salt and pepper. Top with chopped cashews and cilantro and serve with lime wedges.

[serves 4]

Oven-Smoked Spareribs

Indoor smokers are gaining in popularity—if you have one, you have probably discovered how great they are. If you don't have one, it is very easy to create your own by using a few readily available kitchen pans. However, at the minimal cost of a smoker, I encourage everyone to purchase one.

3 pounds (1.4 kg) pork spare ribs, cut into serving-size pieces

1/2 cup (55 g) Sweet Chile Rub (recipe follows)

2 cups (500 g) Molasses BBQ Shmear (recipe follows)

SWEET CHILE RUB

Makes about 1 cup (220 g)

1/2 cup (100 g) sugar

1/4 cup (60 g) light brown sugar

1 tablespoon (7 g) dried mustard

2 tablespoons (18 g) chile powder

1 tablespoon (9 g) chipotle chile powder (may substitute ancho chile powder for a milder taste)

1 tablespoon (18 g) salt

2 tablespoons (12 g) coarsely ground black pepper

MOLASSES BBQ SHMEAR

Makes about 1 1/2 cups (375 g)

4 strips thick-sliced bacon, cut into 1/4" (6.25-mm) slivers

1 large onion, finely chopped (about 2 cups [320 g])

1/2 green bell pepper, finely chopped (about 1 cup [120 g])

2 cloves garlic, minced

1/3 cup (115 g) molasses

1/4 cup (65 g) prepared barbecue sauce

1/4 cup (60 g) ketchup

3 tablespoons (45 g) dark brown sugar

1 tablespoon (15 ml) Worcestershire sauce

1 tablespoon (15 g) prepared mustard

1 tablespoon (15 ml) cider vinegar

1/2 teaspoon (2.5 ml) liquid smoke

1/2 teaspoon (3 g) salt

1 teaspoon (2 g) freshly ground black pepper

Preheat oven to 350°F (180°C, or gas mark 4). Place your indoor smoker over medium heat, with 2 tablespoons (15 g) alder wood chips in the bottom. Place the drip pan in the smoker and fill with 1 cup (235 ml) water; cover with the food rack. Generously rub all the ribs on all sides with the Sweet Chile Rub. Place the ribs on the food rack of the smoker in an even layer and close the lid. Smoke on your stovetop for 30 minutes. Transfer to oven and bake for 1 1/2 hours. Remove from oven, drain smoker, toss hot ribs in 1 1/2 cups (375 g) Molasses BBQ Shmear. Return to food rack of smoker and bake, uncovered, an additional 35 minutes, basting occasionally with the remaining 1/2 cup (125 g) of Molasses BBQ Shmear. Remove from oven and serve hot.

[For Sweet Chile Rub]
Sweet rubs are best on pork and poultry; however, beef ribs are an excellent choice for a sweet dry rub followed by a tart and tangy barbecue sauce. This sweet rub also packs a punch with the addition of hot chile and chipotle powders.

Combine all ingredients in a mixing bowl, stirring to mix well. Dry rub can be stored in an airtight container for up to 1 month.

[For Molasses BBQ Shmear]
A shmear, by my definition, is a thick and chunky barbecue sauce that packs a lot of flavor as a marinade or basting sauce. I have combined some great ingredients in this sauce, with the added flavors of bacon and onion, to offer a great shmear for ribs, beef, poultry, and chicken.

In a heavy pot, cook the bacon over medium heat to render the fat, about 5 minutes. Discard all but 3 tablespoons (45 ml) bacon grease, saving bacon for another use. Add the onion, pepper, and garlic and cook until the vegetables are soft, about 5 minutes. Stir in the molasses, barbecue sauce, ketchup, sugar, Worcestershire sauce, mustard, vinegar, and liquid smoke; season with salt and black pepper. Simmer the sauce, uncovered, for 5 minutes, stirring occasionally. Remove from heat and let cool completely. Sauce can be covered and refrigerated for up to 2 weeks.

[serves 6]

Indian Peppered-Pork Medallions

Indian cooking is robust, with a depth of flavor enhanced by pungent spices. Pork is a great meat for braising, which is done here with paprika, thyme, turmeric, peppers, and tomatoes, creating an almost stewlike consistency. This is excellent as a meal over rice or polenta.

3 tablespoons (45 ml) olive oil

2 pounds (905 g) pork loin steaks (six 5-ounce [140 g] steaks)

Salt and freshly ground black pepper

1 onion, chopped

1 red bell pepper, seeded and sliced thin

1 green bell pepper, seeded and sliced thin

1 yellow or orange bell pepper, seeded and sliced thin

1 red thai chile pepper, seeded and minced

2 tablespoons (16 g) all-purpose flour

3 cloves garlic, sliced thin

1 cup (235 ml) chicken or vegetable stock

1 can (14 ounces [400 g]) chopped tomatoes

2 sprigs fresh thyme

2 bay leaves

1 teaspoon (2.5 g) paprika

1 teaspoon (2 g) turmeric

Preheat oven to 400°F (200°C, or gas mark 6). Heat 2 tablespoons (30 ml) of the olive oil in a large ovenproof skillet over medium-high heat until hot. Season the pork steaks with salt and black pepper. Add to the oil and brown on both sides, 4 minutes per side. Transfer to a plate and set aside. Add remaining tablespoon (15 ml) of oil to the skillet. Once hot, add onion and peppers; sauté until tender, about 5 minutes. Sprinkle with flour, stirring to combine, and cook for 2 minutes. Add the garlic and stock, stirring to thicken; add the tomatoes and bring to a boil. Add the thyme, bay leaves, paprika, and turmeric; season with salt and pepper; stir to combine. Return the pork to the skillet, placing on top of the sauce. Transfer to oven and bake for 45 minutes, until pork is tender. Remove bay leaves and thyme sprigs and serve with potatoes, rice, or polenta.

[serves 8]

Polenta Lasagna **with Linguica and Swiss Chard**

Polenta is such a versatile food. In this recipe I have prepared it to a rich, creamy texture, flavored it with Parmesan cheese, and allowed it to cool for use in place of lasagna noodles. The polenta layers, the robust flavor of linguica, and the delicate nature of the Swiss chard go well together.

POLENTA

2 cups (475 ml) milk

1 tablespoon (14 g) unsalted butter

1/2 teaspoon (3 g) salt

1 teaspoon (2.5 g) sugar

1 cup (135 g) stone-ground yellow cornmeal or fine yellow grits

1/4 cup (25 g) grated Parmesan cheese

FILLING

4 tablespoons (55 g) unsalted butter

4 tablespoons (55 ml) olive oil

1 medium yellow onion, finely chopped

1 carrot, peeled and finely chopped

1 celery stalk, finely chopped

2 cloves garlic, chopped

1/2 pound (225 g) linguica or chorizo chopped to 1/4" (6 mm) dice

1/2 cup (120 ml) dry red wine

1 (14-ounce [425 ml]) can diced tomatoes with purée

1/4 teaspoon (.5 g) red pepper flakes

Salt and freshly cracked black pepper

SWISS CHARD PUREE

1 bunch (about 1 pound [455 g]) Swiss chard, washed, patted dry, and roughly chopped

1/2 cup (75 g) crumbled feta cheese

1/2 teaspoon (1.25 g) freshly ground nutmeg

1/4 teaspoon (.5 g) ground ginger

2 cloves garlic, minced

3 tablespoons (7.5 g) fresh basil, minced

1 teaspoon (1.3 g) fresh flat-leaf parsley, minced

1/2 cup (120 ml) heavy cream

1/2 pound (225 g) fresh mozzarella cheese, sliced

[For polenta]

Combine milk, butter, salt, and sugar in a heavy-bottomed saucepan (a Teflon-coated one works best). Bring to a simmer, just until steaming. Add cornmeal in a steady stream, whisking continuously to combine it and prevent lumps from forming. Once combined, reduce the heat to a simmer and continue to cook, stirring continuously, until the mixture is thick and begins to pull away from the sides of the pot, about 2 to 5 minutes. Remove from the heat and add the Parmesan cheese. Combine thoroughly.

Oil a 10" × 15" (25 x 37.5 cm) sheet pan. Pour the polenta into the prepared pan, spreading it flat with an oiled spatula. Cool until firm, about 1 hour. (The polenta can be made up to a day ahead. Cover the pan with plastic wrap and refrigerate it.)

[For sausage filling]

In a large saucepan over medium heat, melt 2 tablespoons (28 g) butter with 2 tablespoons (28 ml) of olive oil. Add the onion, carrot, and celery, and cook, stirring, until tender but not browned, about 10 minutes. Stir in the garlic. Add the sausage and cook, stirring, until browned, about 10 minutes. Add the wine and cook until the liquid evaporates, about 2 additional minutes. Add the tomatoes and their juice, the parsley, and the red pepper flakes. Stir to combine. Season with salt and pepper, and reduce the heat to a simmer. Simmer uncovered until the mixture is thickened, about 30 minutes.

[For Swiss chard puree]
In a medium saucepan, heat the remaining 2 tablespoons (28 g) of butter with the remaining 2 tablespoons (28 ml) of olive oil. Add the Swiss chard, tossing to coat with oil. Cover and let steam until the chard is tender and bright green in color, about 5 minutes. Stir occasionally to ensure that the chard is tender. Remove the saucepan from the heat and set it aside. Preheat the oven to 400°F (200°C, or gas mark 6). Oil a 9" × 13" (22.5 x 32.5 cm) baking dish. In a food processor, combine the chard, feta cheese, nutmeg, ginger, garlic, basil, and parsley. Process the mixture until pureed. Add the cream, scrape down the sides, and process the mixture until it is well combined and creamy.

[To assemble]
Remove the polenta from the refrigerator. Cut the polenta into twelve equal squares. Arrange half of the squares in the bottom of the baking dish. Spoon on half of the Swiss chard puree, coating the polenta evenly. Top the puree with half of the sausage mixture. Top the

sausage with half of the fresh mozzarella cheese slices. Repeat the layers using the remaining ingredients. Bake until the cheese melts and the sauce is bubbling, about 30 minutes. Let stand for 5 minutes before serving. Serve hot, directly from the oven.

[serves 6]

Red Curry Chicken Casserole

This dish was inspired by Asian and Indian cooking. With these cultures' flavors, spices, and textures, this dish is a true "melting pot" of taste.

8 tablespoons (120 ml) peanut oil

5 cups (1.2 L) canned coconut milk, thick and thin divided (see Cook's Note)

3 tablespoons (45 g) prepared red curry paste (available in the international foods section of your supermarket)

1 whole chicken, cut into 8 pieces (wings, thighs, legs, breasts)

4 cloves fresh garlic, minced

2 cups (200 g) cauliflower, blanched

2 tablespoons (28 ml) Thai fish sauce

2 tablespoons (28 ml) lime juice

1/2 cup (20 g) basil, chopped

Salt and pepper

2 red chiles (cayenne, serrano, or substitute 1/2 red bell pepper), cut into long, thin strips

Preheat oven to 400°F (200°C, or gas mark 6). Heat 2 tablespoons (28 ml) of oil in a large, heavy-bottomed sauce pot over medium-high heat. Add 1/2 cup (120 ml) of the thicker coconut milk. When bubbling, add the curry paste and cook, stirring, for 2 minutes, then add remaining 1/2 cup (120 ml) thicker milk, cooking for 5 to 8 minutes, until the oil begins to separate. Remove from heat and set aside to cool. In a large mixing bowl, toss the chicken with 2 tablespoons (28 ml) peanut oil and the garlic. Heat 2 tablespoons (28 ml) peanut oil in a 13" (32.5-cm) ovenproof skillet over medium-high heat, place the chicken pieces in a single layer in the hot skillet, turning to sear and brown on all sides, about 7 minutes. Remove from skillet and set aside to cool. In the same skillet, heat remaining 2 tablespoons (28 ml) peanut oil, add the blanched cauliflower, and brown for 5 minutes. Return the chicken to the pan with cauliflower. In a large bowl, combine coconut-curry milk with remaining 4 cups (9,464 ml) thin coconut milk, fish sauce, lime juice, and basil. Season with salt and pepper, pour over chicken and cauliflower, sprinkle with peppers. Place in hot oven and bake for 45 minutes. Remove and serve chicken pieces with peppers over rice.

[Cook's Note]
Coconut Milk

When buying a can of coconut milk, resist the urge to shake it. You will notice when you open the can, there are well-defined thick and thin portions of the milk. For this recipe, and many others, it is important to use the milk as it is separated. To remove the thick top layer, just simply use a spoon to scoop it out into a separate bowl.

[serves 4]

Whole Sake Trout with White Beans and Lemon Thyme

Preparing trout whole, as in this recipe, is quite easy and makes for a great presentation at the table. Any seafood market, and quite often specialty food marts, will sell whole trout already cleaned and ready to go. If only fillets are available, use them, reducing the broiling time to around 5 minutes per side.

1 cup (235 ml) pineapple juice

1/2 cup (120 ml) tamari*

1/2 cup (120 ml) mirin*

3/4 cup (175 ml) sake*

1 1/2 tablespoons (9 g) coarsely ground black pepper

1/2 tablespoon (9 g) sea salt

4 whole cleaned trout, heads and tails removed

2 lemons, cut into a total of 8 slices

16 sprigs fresh lemon thyme

3 tablespoons (45 ml) olive oil

1/2 cup (80 g) chopped Vidalia onion

1/2 cup (75 g) chopped red bell pepper

1/2 cup (75 g) chopped green bell pepper

3 cloves fresh garlic, minced

1/2 cup (40 g) chopped portobello mushrooms

1 can (15.5 ounces [439 g]) cannelloni beans, rinsed and drained

2 tablespoons (28 ml) rice vinegar

2 bay leaves

1 pound (455 g) cooked orzo

Prepare the marinade in a large nonreactive bowl by combining the pineapple juice, tamari, mirin, sake, black pepper, and sea salt. Stuff each trout with 2 slices of lemon and 4 sprigs of thyme, place in marinade, cover, and refrigerate for at least 1 hour. Preheat broiler to 475°F (240°C, or gas mark 9). Heat the olive oil in a large stainless steel or cast-iron skillet over medium-high heat. Add the onion, red and green peppers, garlic, and mushrooms; sauté until the onions become tender and translucent, about 8 minutes, stirring occasionally. Add the beans, rice vinegar, and bay leaves; stir to combine, and cook for 4 minutes. Place trout in skillet on top of bean mixture and baste with 1/3 cup (80 ml) marinade. Place under broiler on rack in lower third of oven, and cook for 8 minutes, until skin begins to buckle and brown. Turn fish and baste with an additional 1/3 cup (80 ml) marinade; broil for 8 more

minutes. Remove bay leaves and serve fish over orzo, topping with bean mixture and a drizzle of pan sauce. Instruct your guests to remove the skin using the tine of a fork and be careful of bones when eating. The flesh of the fish should fall from the bone, making it easy to remove the entire bone structure in one whole piece.

Tamari (a soy sauce), mirin, and sake (rice wines) are available in the international foods section of the grocery store or in specialty food shops

[Cook's Note]
A Note on Trout

Trout is a widely popular fish from the same family as salmon and whitefish. With many different varieties from both fresh and salt water (fresh being the most popular), trout can grow to larger sizes but is typically found in the 8- to 12-ounce (225- to 340-g) range popular for grilling, frying, and broiling. Rainbow trout is the most recognized trout, with an irridescent skin displaying a rainbow-colored effect. Brook and speckled trout are considered the best eating because of their mild flavor and hearty texture.

Index

Acknowledgments

As with all of my books, there are many people who contribute to creating the final product, the results of which I am very proud. I would like to thank, again, Rockport Publishers for giving me the opportunity to share my recipes and culinary thoughts. I would like to thank several individuals immensely for their guidance, patience, fortitude, craftsmanship, and belief in me and my work: Winnie Prentiss, publisher and patient guide; Rochelle Bourgault, editorial project manager; Rosalind Wanke, art director; David Martinell, design project manager; Allan Penn, photographer; and Liz Polay-Wettengel, publicist. Thank you, as well, to my friends and family who always encourage me to give my best.

As usual, thank you to all who choose my books to read and use as tools in the kitchen.

Enjoy!

About the Author

Dwayne Ridgaway, a native of Kerrville, Texas, currently resides in Bristol, Rhode Island. He is the author of the well-received *Lasagna: The Art of Layered Cooking; Pizza: 50 Traditional and Alternative Recipes for the Oven and the Grill; Sandwiches, Panini, and Wraps: Recipes for the Original "Anytime, Anywhere" Meal;* and *Indoor Grilling: 50 Recipes for Electric Grills, Stovetop Grills, and Smokers.* He is also a contributing author, food stylist, and recipe developer for several notable magazines and books. Dwayne, a graduate of the highly respected Johnson and Wales University, currently works in Rhode Island as a food and beverage consultant, caterer, and event designer. He has, in short, made a career out of exploring and celebrating the culinary arts. His passion is fresh ingredients and new flavors, which give him the ability to develop new and exciting recipes that any reader can execute and enjoy. Dwayne's goal is for all readers to use his recipes and writing as a groundwork for their own personal creativity.